The Sampler Book

D1761505

Also by the Authors
LAMP MAKING
NEEDLECRAFT MANUAL

The Sampler Book

by Ana G. Lopo and Bruce W. Murphy

CROWN PUBLISHERS, INC., NEW YORK

©1978 by Ana G. Lopo and Bruce W. Murphy
All rights reserved. No part of this book may be reproduced or utilized
in any form or by any means, electronic or mechanical, including
photocopying, recording, or by any information storage and retrieval
system, without permission in writing from the publisher.
Inquiries should be addressed to Crown Publishers, Inc., One Park Avenue,
New York, N.Y. 10016
Printed in the United States of America
Published simultaneously in Canada by
General Publishing Company Limited

Library of Congress Cataloging in Publication Data

Lopo, Ana G.
  The sampler book.

  Bibliography: p.
  Includes index.
  1. Embroidery. 2. Samplers. I. Murphy,
Bruce W., joint author. II. Title.
TT775.L66   746.3   78-9465

ISBN 0-517-53461-4

CONTENTS

acknowledgments

We would like to thank some very special people who gave their time generously to help us complete this book. We would especially like to thank our talented friends Barbara Egner and Judy Thompson who enthusiastically embroidered two beautiful samplers. Our special thanks to Mrs. Eva Egner and Tove Simonsen for lending us several needlework projects.

Our most sincere thanks to Rebecca Simon, director of the Burlington Historical Society, and to William W. Cleland, also of the society, for sharing their knowledge and time with us. And to Brandt Aymar, a heartfelt thank you for editorial guidance and encouragement.

PREfACE

This book deals with samplers you can make from beginning to end. The six complete iron-on transfer samplers in the back of the book are ready to be transferred and stitched. Several pages of iron-on motifs and alphabets have been designed to let you create many unique samplers.

After reading the history of samplers and studying the sampler photographs, you can decide the style, color scheme, and other details of your project. You can then refer to the 15 complete sampler graphs in the book and start your project.

After the iron-on transfers have been used several times, you can make them a permanent part of your embroidery design collection by copying them on graph paper.

1 | A brief history of the sampler

What is a sampler? Newcomers to antique collecting or needlecraft often ask this question.

The Latin word "exemplar," meaning model, gave the needlework sampler its name. We can go as far back as the Renaissance, when embroidery was at its peak in Europe, to get to the meaning of the word.

Well-bred women of the sixteenth century were able to embroider household articles and clothing with exquisite designs that we can see in museums and collections today.

Queens and noble ladies took to this art with tremendous enthusiasm, executing intricate Jacobean flowers and cut-lace work to complement bed linens, shirt ruffles, and cushions. Embroidered articles were treasured in the Elizabethan period—a portrait of Queen Elizabeth I of England shows a number of plants and animals embroidered on the front panel of her skirt. These symbolized the prosperity of her reign and success of her explorers across the seas.

And Mary Queen of Scots spent her captive hours embroidering and talking with the ladies who accompanied her.

In order to keep records of their favorite embroidery patterns at a time when paper was scarce, ladies embroidered them on linen swatches and referred to them when necessary. These swatches were the original samplers, and recording embroidery patterns was the reason they came into existence.

The earliest record of a sampler mentioned in literature was made by the poet Skelton (1460-1529), who speaks of the "sampler to sowe on, the laces to embroide." In 1552 it is already an item valuable enough to be listed in an inventory of Edward VI. The inventory lists a parchment book that contains "item: Sampler or set of patterns worked on Normandy Canvas."

The earliest samplers, in the sixteenth century, consisted of scattered embroidery motifs and lacework patterns executed on a long, unhemmed, narrow piece of cloth. According to experts, the early European sampler shape was dictated by the narrow width of the loom; and its considerable length—sometimes up to three feet—was a result of joining pieces of cloth when the original piece was full (Fig. 1).

Perhaps because of their odd shape and

1

Fig. 1. Sixteenth-century samplers were long and narrow.

While sixteenth-century samplers consisted of motifs and cut-lace work scattered at random on the cloth, seventeenth-century samplers begin to show a pattern of design. Embroidery stitches and cut and drawn work patterns were grouped—often with lace patterns at the bottom and embroidery at the top—on a narrow piece of fabric often hemmed on all sides. This shape worked out well, since the width of approximately 9 inches allowed for one horizontal band of stitches with the repeat design appearing two or three times. The next line was a different band of stitches, and so on down the length of the piece.

American Samplers

The first American samplers were influenced by seventeenth-century English pieces. Because they were highly valued and easily transported, many settlers carried their samplers to the New World, perhaps hoping to use them as a source of inspiration or perhaps just for sentimental reasons.

The earliest American works include Anne Gower's sampler. She became the wife of Massachusetts' Governor Endecott, before 1628. Her sampler, dated by experts at approximately 1610, was embroidered in England. However, later it was brought to America and is claimed, with much controversy, as an American sampler today.

Loara Standish, daughter of Pilgrim Captain Myles Standish, holds the honor to the present date of stitching the first American-made sampler. It has been dated at approximately 1640, and it is worked in embroidered bands of flowers, followed by a verse:

> Loara Standish is my name,
> Lord guide my heart that I may do thy will
> As I will conduce to virtue devoid of shame
> And I will give glory to thy name.

In the eighteenth-century American sampler we begin to see the use of borders, implying that the sampler was planned as a needlework

because they were used only for reference, these samplers were rolled and stored in sampler boxes or trunks, instead of being framed and displayed.

piece rather than as a tool to record scattered motifs and patterns. Samplers began to transform from the long and narrow shape that had prevailed into the square piece we know today (Fig. 2).

basic in design (alphabets and numerals) (Fig. 3); and finishing school samplers, which were made by older girls and were more elaborate in design (Fig. 4).

Fig. 2. Unfinished sampler. *Courtesy Burlington Historical Society, Burlington, New Jersey*

Fig. 3. Alphabet sampler completed in 1824. *Courtesy Burlington Historical Society, Burlington, New Jersey*

Early in the eighteenth century, the sampler was used to teach young girls the alphabet and numbers, again evidence that it was no longer needed as a record alone. Irregularities are characteristic of the eighteenth-century sampler—borders are not centered, motifs are asymmetrical, and corners do not match.

Also in that century, schools opened to educate girls in the art of needlework. American samplers created at needlework schools fall into two categories: Dame school samplers, which young children produced and are very

The use of certain motifs and patterns enables us to trace the origin of many samplers to needlework schools or geographical areas of the country.

Signed and dated samplers with a verse or alphabet enclosed within a frame of leaves and vines stitched in black, tan, or pale blue silk are typical of the Westtown Boarding School in Chester County, Pennsylvania.

Samplers consisting of darning designs have also originated in the Westtown School. The need to repair worn clothing was responsible for the development of this type of sampler.

The first recorded border was made by eight-year-old Mary Daintery of New Haven, Connec-

Fig. 4. Deborah F. Wire's sampler was completed in Burlington, New Jersey, in 1823. Four alphabets, verse, and scattered motifs with a four-sided border. *Photo courtesy Burlington Historical Society, Burlington, New Jersey*

Fig. 5. Adam and Eve characters are a detail from Adam and Eve Sampler project by Judy Thompson.

Fig. 6. Martha Kirby's sampler is 21" x 16". It contains several verses and a pictorial at the bottom, which includes a house, farm animals, butterflies, robins, and trees exquisitely stitched. *Photo courtesy Burlington Historical Society, James Fenimore Cooper House, Burlington, New Jersey*

ticut, in 1721. And pieces illustrated with Adam and Eve characters made an appearance in 1741 near Boston (Fig. 5).

Near the second half of the eighteenth century we find that American samplers diverted from conventional designs; creative scenes with trees, animals, and figures were boldly executed by girls at home and school. Perspective was lacking (flowers towered over people, giant butterflies danced in the sky), but the results were exceptionally beautiful (Fig. 6).

Proud parents framed and exhibited their youngsters' handiwork on the main wall of the sitting room or parlor (Figs. 7 and 8).

Mourning samplers were neglected and overlooked by needlework experts and collectors, perhaps because of their somber nature.

Fig. 7. Amy Kirby's sampler measures 11″ x 10½″ and contains willow trees and a house embroidered in cross-stitch. *Courtesy Burlington Historical Society, Burlington, New Jersey; photo Bruce Murphy*

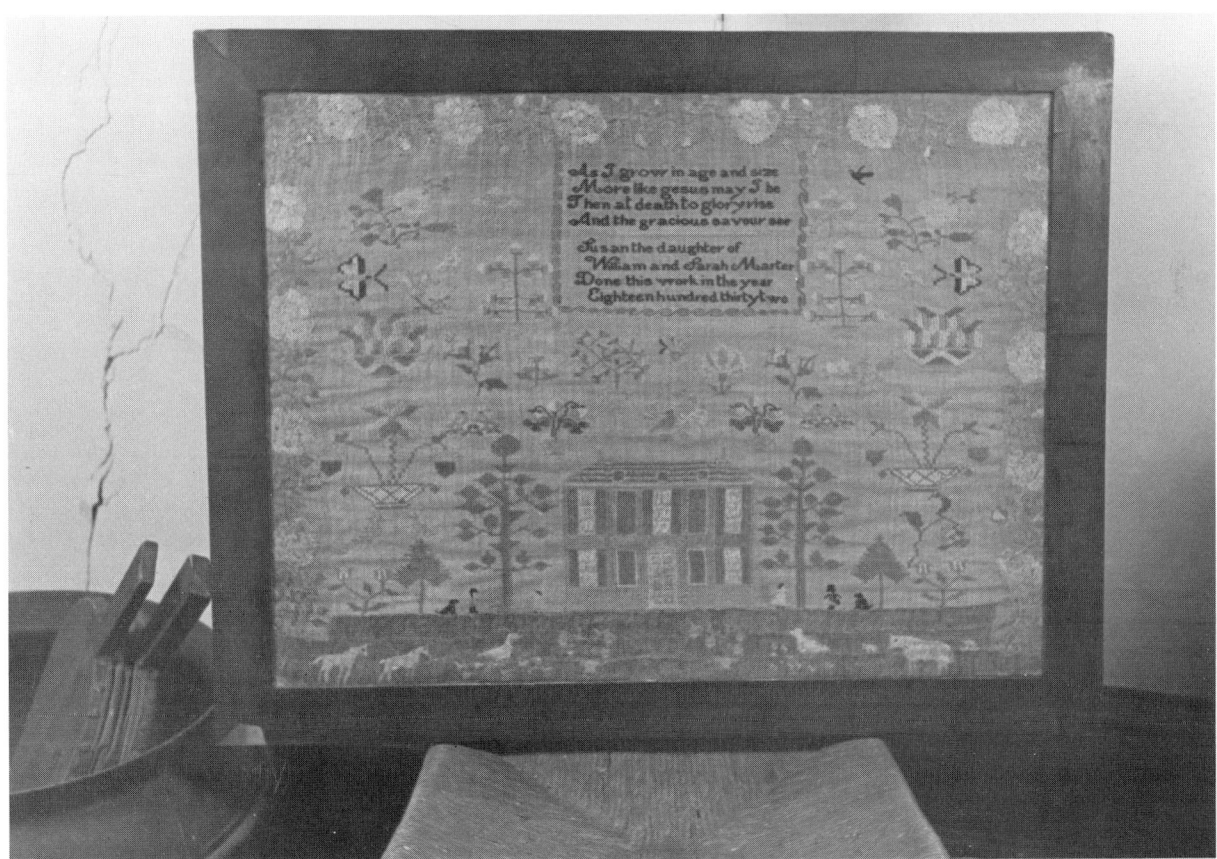

Fig. 8. Susan Marter's beautiful sampler was completed in 1832. She stitched farm animals, butterflies, and a three-sided border of large flowers. A house, with five windows executed in an attractive darning stitch, is the central motif. She used satin, cross, running, and stem stitches on her sampler. *Photo courtesy Burlington Historical Society, Burlington, New Jersey; photo by Bruce Murphy*

These pictorial embroideries usually involved patient stitching and painting on silk.

The technical sequence of these embroideries is believed to be first sketching the designs on silk, then embroidering some elements, and finally painting the rest.

The memorial embroideries often included the following elements: a monument, weeping relatives, weeping trees, and water. Embroidery on silk is difficult, and particularly stitching on the face and hands. So these were usually painted (Fig. 9).

This art was popular from 1800 to 1815 and then suffered a decline. The first memorial pieces appeared after the death of George Washington in 1799, mostly in New York, Pennsylvania, New England, and the Middle Atlantic states.

The nineteenth-century sampler is a very individual piece of needlework. Most samplers display the creativity of their makers.

Among some interesting nineteenth-century works are map samplers. Although they were popular in England, they never really caught on in America. Few schools in New York, New

Fig. 10. Perforated cardboard embroidery, celebrating the nation's centennial. *Courtesy Burlington Historical Society, Burlington, New Jersey; photo by Bruce Murphy*

Fig. 9. Mourning sampler.

England, and the South are credited with creating American map samplers. They were usually worked with black silk outline stitch on a pale satin cloth. Their appearance coincides with the time when geography was added to a school's curricula, and many experts believe they served as a geography teaching and learning tool. Embroidered globes can be traced, almost exclusively, to the Westtown School near Philadelphia.

Another development of the nineteenth century is commercial perforated cardboard. The cardboard was used as a background for satin and cross-stitches (Fig. 10). This example of perforated cardboard embroidery was completed in celebration of the nation's centennial.

We also see family record samplers appearing late in the eighteenth century and becoming very popular in the nineteenth century.

Fig. 11. This unfinished sampler is 10¼" x 11¼". A Berlin pattern-type garland of roses is combined with an alphabet. *Courtesy Burlington Historical Society, Burlington, New Jersey; photo Bruce Murphy*

Sampler Motifs and Designs through the Centuries

Ribbons. A ribbon around the edges of a sampler, either plain or gathered, can be traced to Pennsylvania. To a lesser extent some New England and English samplers also are "framed" in ribbons (Fig. 12). The ribbons were usually in contrasting colors or the same color as the sampler.

Basket of Flowers. This particular basket of flowers design appears, with some variations, in samplers from Trenton, New Jersey, and Pennsylvania (Fig. 13).

Fig. 12. Mary Crispin's sampler is 18" x 19" and has a gathered ribbon border. *Courtesy Burlington Historical Society, Burlington, New Jersey; photo by Bruce Murphy*

These family records sometimes consisted of embroidered trees with the name and date of birth of family members stitched inside its leaves or fruit. When a person died, the date of death was stitched in black under it.

The American eagle appears on several samplers late in the nineteenth century, but these are rare.

Most experts agree that the deterioration of needlework in America started after 1830. Some claim that it was due to women's education in more academic subjects. Others blame the Berlin woolwork style for destroying the individuality of the sampler.

The Berlin woolwork period, which began around 1820, has been singled out by many as the main factor responsible for the deterioration of American samplers. Berlin patterns were hand-painted stitch graphs imported from Germany, which could be followed easily for wool or silk embroidery on canvas. Berlin patterns were suitable for shading, eliminating the flat but enchanting American designs.

Some samplers combined Berlin woolwork with traditional elements such as alphabets (Fig. 11).

Fig. 13. Detail of the Trenton Sampler by Bruce Murphy.

Angular Borders. Pennsylvania German samplers usually have a stiff, angular border on three sides or four sides (Fig. 14).

Pennsylvania German Motifs. Most Pennsylvania German samplers are not pictorial. Although balanced, motifs are usually very angular and include peacocks and birds in cross-stitch with minimal amounts of free embroidery (Fig. 15).

An Emblem of Love Motif. This motif, usually an octagon with a pair of birds and the words "An Emblem of Love," is often seen in Trenton, New Jersey, samplers and in samplers from Pennsylvania (Fig. 16).

Crinkly Silk. Home-dyed, these came in a thick twist that was unrolled to use separate strands for embroidery. This gave it the crinkly look found in many American samplers. The thread was used to embroider grass, flower petals, and other elements (Fig. 17).

Floral Wreaths. These were used in the nineteenth century to encircle the verse or name in samplers with no other elaborate designs (Fig. 18).

Architectural Samplers. Public buildings, churches, and schools were popular motifs in the nineteenth century. The schoolhouse sampler, as it is sometimes called, consists of a single building either alone or integrated into the landscape. It often represented the building of the school where the sampler originated (Figs. 19 and 20).

Contemporary Samplers. Contemporary wall hangings can be designed with an easy cross-

Fig. 14. Border of Ana's Sampler by A. G. Lopo.

Fig. 15. Detail of Mary Ann's sampler. The central motif of this 16″ x 21″ sampler is a swan centered between two giant sunflowers. *Courtesy Burlington Historical Society, Burlington, New Jersey*

Fig. 16. Graph of "Emblem of Love" motif.

stitch arrangement. This Danish sampler was made by Tove Simonsen (Figs. 21 and 22).

Samplers as Gifts. Early in the twentieth century, samplers were often made as gifts for weddings, trips, and other occasions. This sampler was made as a parting gift by Mrs.

Katie Wolf to her sister. It reads: "Many long years will pass until we see each other again, Remain a dear sister over there as you were here" (Fig. 23).

Shading in Embroidery. The shading influence that started in nineteenth-century Europe is evident in this cross-stitch sampler by Mrs. Eva Egner (Fig. 24).

Fig. 17. Crimped floss silk thread was generally used in the United States but seldom elsewhere. *Courtesy Burlington Historical Society, Burlington, New Jersey*

Fig. 18. Open floral border encloses Elizabeth Welling's sampler completed in 1833. *Courtesy Burlington Historical Society, Burlington, New Jersey*

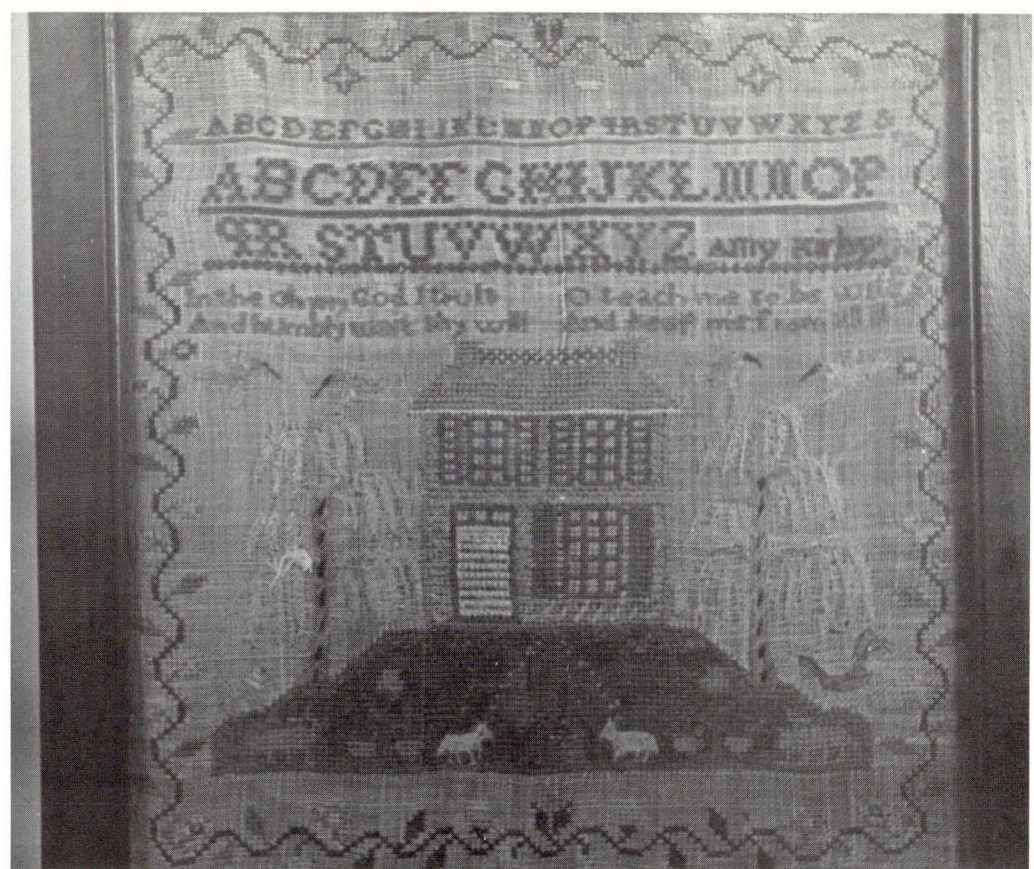

Fig. 19. Detail of house in Amy Kirby's sampler. *Courtesy Burlington Historical Society, Burlington, New Jersey*

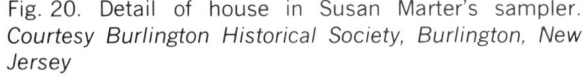

Fig. 20. Detail of house in Susan Marter's sampler. *Courtesy Burlington Historical Society, Burlington, New Jersey*

Fig. 21. Danish sampler by Tove Simonsen. *Photo by Bruce Murphy*

Fig. 22. Detail of Tove Simonsen's sampler.

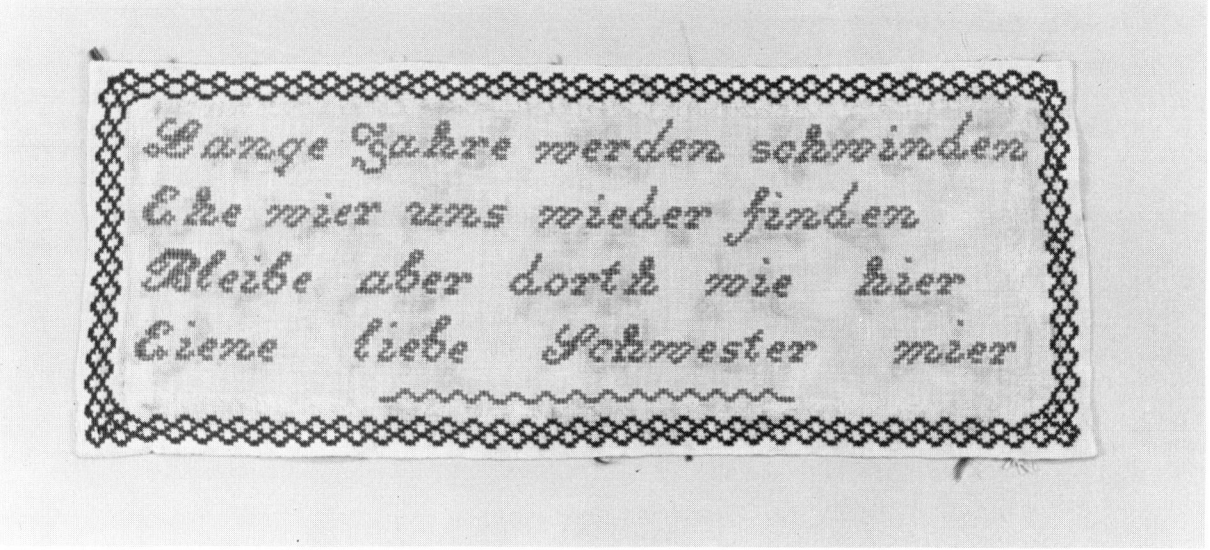

Fig. 23. Sampler by Mrs. Katie Wolf.

Fig. 24. Cross-stitched scene by Mrs. Eva Egner.

Symbolism and Sampler Motifs

The significance of sampler motifs can be very intriguing. The following list of traditional symbols and their meaning will give you a general idea you might find useful when designing samplers.

ANIMALS

Peacock. Vanity, ostentation, luxury, pride.
Dove. Peace, gentleness, messenger of love.
Paired Birds. Facing or opposed to each other, good and evil, day and night, summer and winter, and other opposites.
Duck. Fidelity.
Rooster. Conquerer, watchfulness.
Turtle. Slowness and strength.
Snake. Evil, temptation.
Butterfly. Immortality, joy, pleasure, and inconstancy.
Parrot. Talkative, gossip.
Swan. According to German mythology it is the sign of light and life. It is a bird of love.
Dog. Fidelity, loyalty, wrath, and envy.
Cat. Independency, idleness, coquetry.
Owl. Wisdom, the devil.

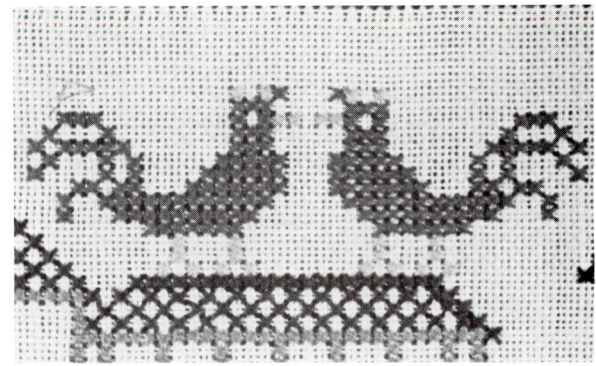

Fig. 26.

Fig. 27.

Fig. 25.

Fig. 28.

Fig. 29.

Fig. 30.

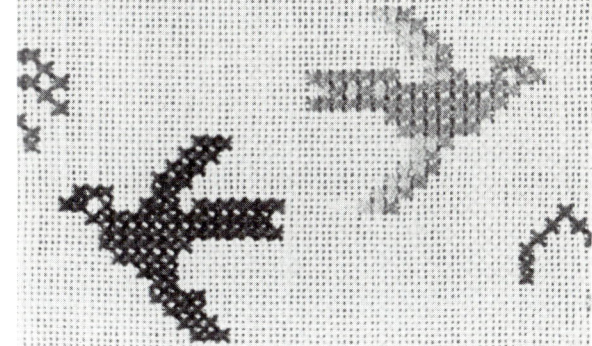

Fig. 32.

Fig. 31.

PEOPLE

Adam and Eve. Good and evil.
Angels with Trumpets. Heavenly voice announcing the Day of Judgment.
Angels Holding Palm Leaves. Victory.

Fig. 33.

Fig. 36.

Fig. 34.

Fig. 35.

Fig. 37.

Fig. 38.

Fig. 39.

Fig. 40.

TREES

Tree of Life. Used by Pennsylvania Germans in many of their samplers. Its raised branches symbolize the new life. It is embroidered growing from a basket or directly from the soil.

Weeping Willow. The tree of sorrow and death. It also gives comfort to those in grief.

Oak Tree/Leaf. Sign of strength.

Palm Branches. Life.

Apple Tree. Love and fertility; temptation.

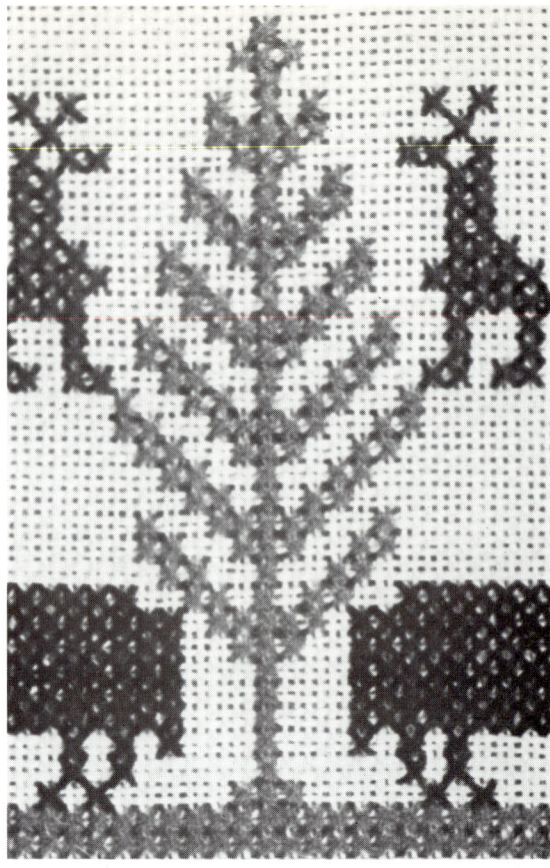

Fig. 42.

Fig. 41.

Fig. 43.

Fig. 44.

18

Fig. 45.

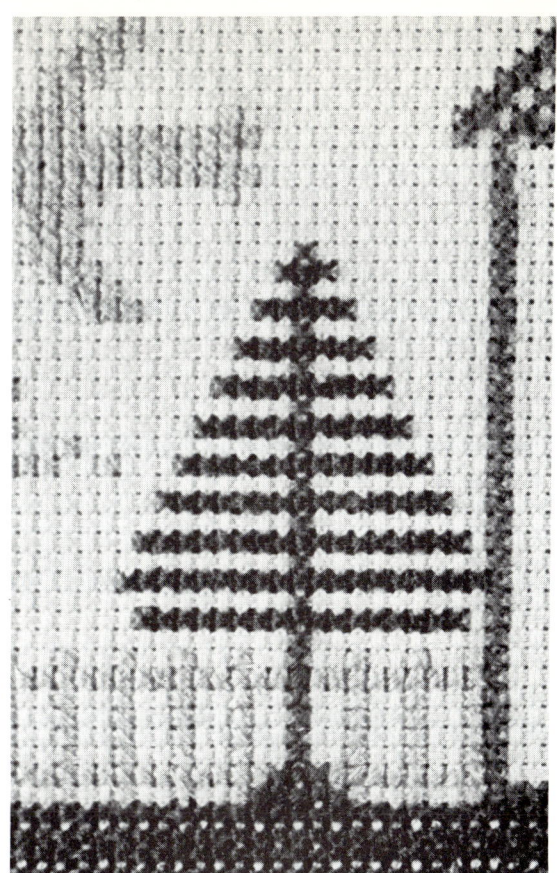

Fig. 47.

Fig. 48.

Fig. 46.

FLOWERS

Tulip. Symbolizes the Trinity.
Lily. Purity, fertility.
Violet. Humility, modesty.
Rose. Used seldom in profile or bud, but in full face, as a single flower. It is the symbol of the universal flower and beauty.
Carnation. Frequently used in Persian ornamentation.

Fig. 50.

Fig. 52.

Fig. 49..

Fig. 51.

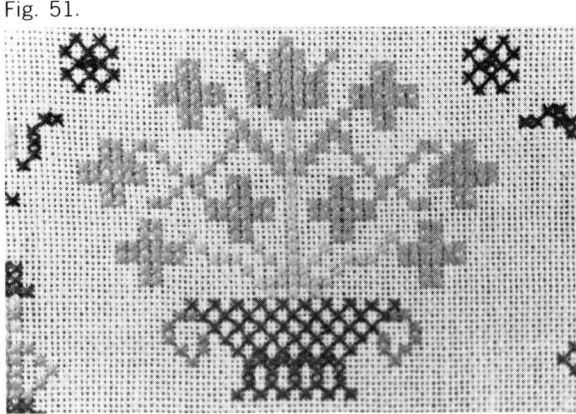

Fig. 53.

Mary Ann Austin's work A D

Fig. 54.

Fig. 55.

Fig. 56.

ARCHITECTURE

Buildings. These have, as far as we know, no symbolic meaning but rather a representative meaning. Often the buildings represented the school where the sampler was worked, a church, or home. Some public buildings such as poorhouses, universities, and museums were also popular subjects for samplers.

Fig. 58.

Fig. 57.

Fig. 59.

Fig. 61.

Fig. 60.

OTHER

Crowns. Used often in Tudor decoration. Not usually found in American samplers, except those of Pennsylvania Germans. Crowns were used mostly to fill up spaces left after completing an alphabet, or were scattered among other designs. In Europe they were used also to indicate rank of the nobility.

Ships. Representative of ships in American samplers. Also symbolizing safe travel.

Wavy Lines. Used sometimes as part of borders, symbolizing water and day and night.

Sampler Borders

Late in the first half of the eighteenth century, about 1725, the border became a frame for the sampler. It included matching corners.

Earlier borders are embroidered in cross-stitch and follow the popular angular designs. Simple strawberry, rose, tulip, and carnation borders appear. These gave way to the flower sprays and graceful floral borders of forget-me-nots and roses.

In the nineteenth century we find grapevines and morning glories gracing the borders.

Several borders are illustrated below.

Fig. 63.

Fig. 62.

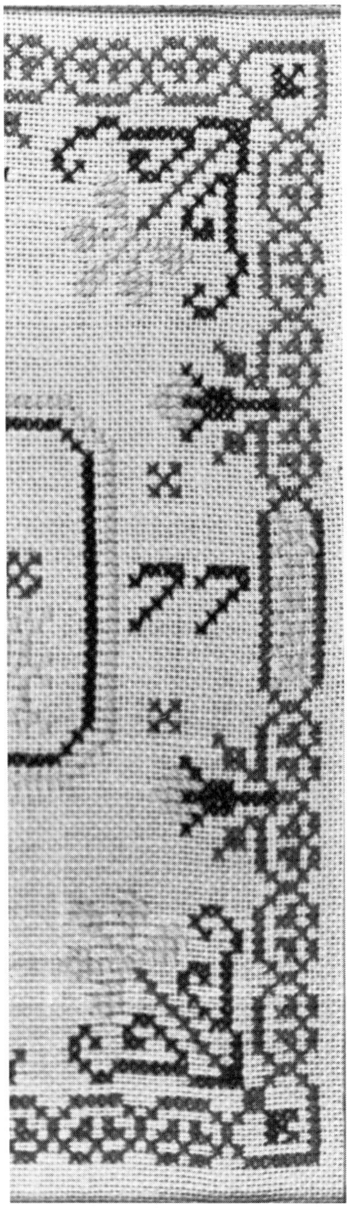

Fig. 64.

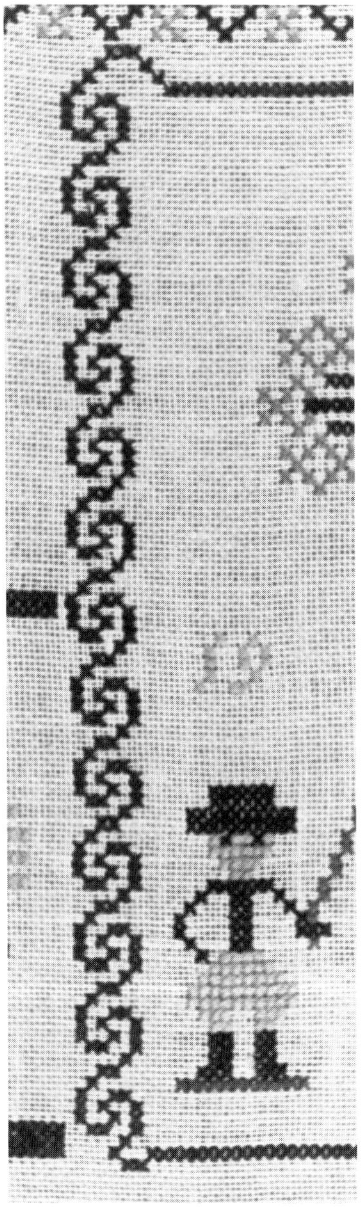

Fig. 66.

Fig. 67.

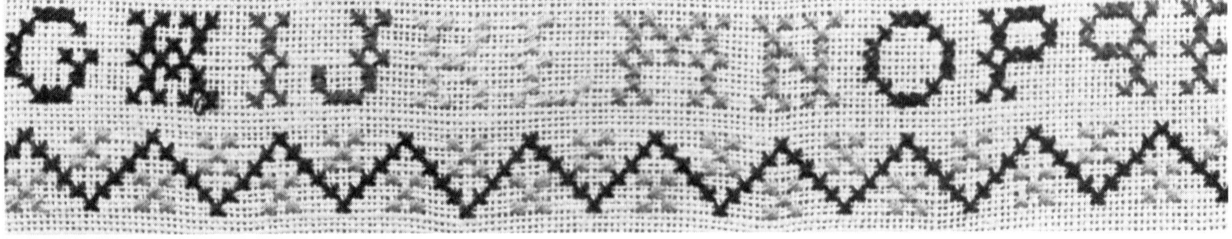

Fig. 65.

Trenton Sampler. By Bruce W. Murphy

Pennsylvania German Compendium Sampler. By Ana G. Lopo

Adam and Eve Sampler.
By Judy Thompson

Ana's Sampler (iron-on 8" x 10"). By Ana G. Lopo

Opposite: Embroidered and painted sampler (iron-on 16" x 20").

Alphabet Sampler. By Bruce W. Murphy

Dutch Sampler (iron-on 8″ x 10″). By Bruce W. Murphy

Nineteenth-Century American Sampler (iron-on 16″ x 20″). By Bruce W. Murphy

Peacock Sampler (iron-on 8" x 10"). By Ana G. Lopo

Farm Sampler. By Bruce W. Murphy

Long Dutch Sampler. By Bruce W. Murphy

Country House Sampler. By Bruce W. Murphy

Angels and Alphabet Sampler (iron-on 8" x 10"). By Bruce W. Murphy

Black Sheep Sampler. By Barbara Egner

Pennsylvania Dutch Heart Sampler. By Ana G. Lopo

Fig. 68.

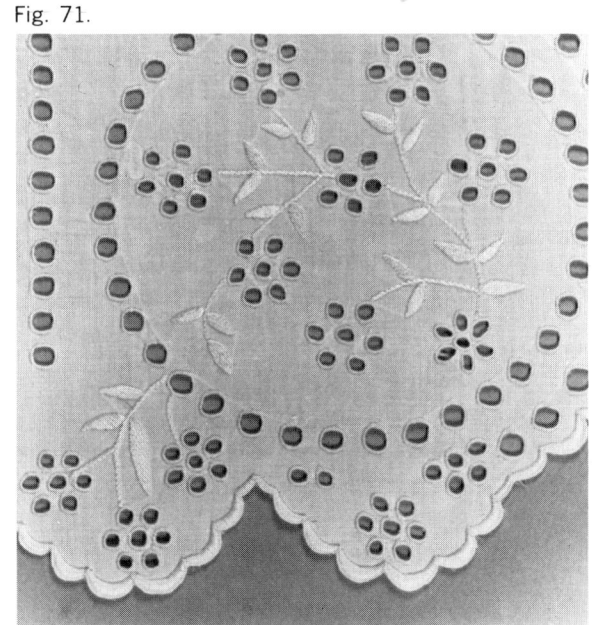

Fig. 70.

Fig. 71.

Fig. 69.

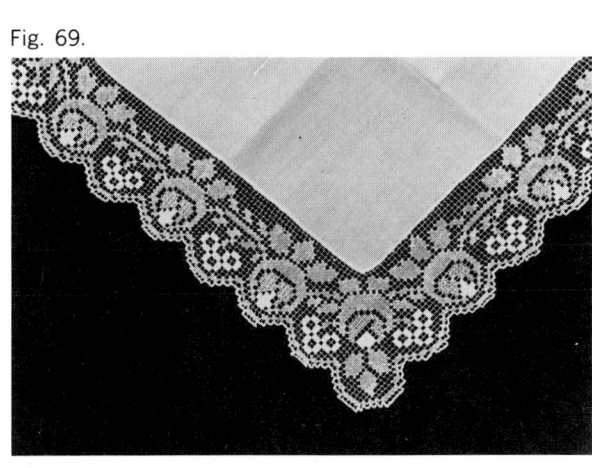

Sampler Alphabets

Omitting letters in an alphabet was common practice. For example, U and V were deleted from many alphabets, since W could serve as a model for stitching both. X, Y, and Z were sometimes deleted because they were not used frequently; J was omitted since I could serve as a model for I and J.

Some alphabet examples follow.

Fig. 74.

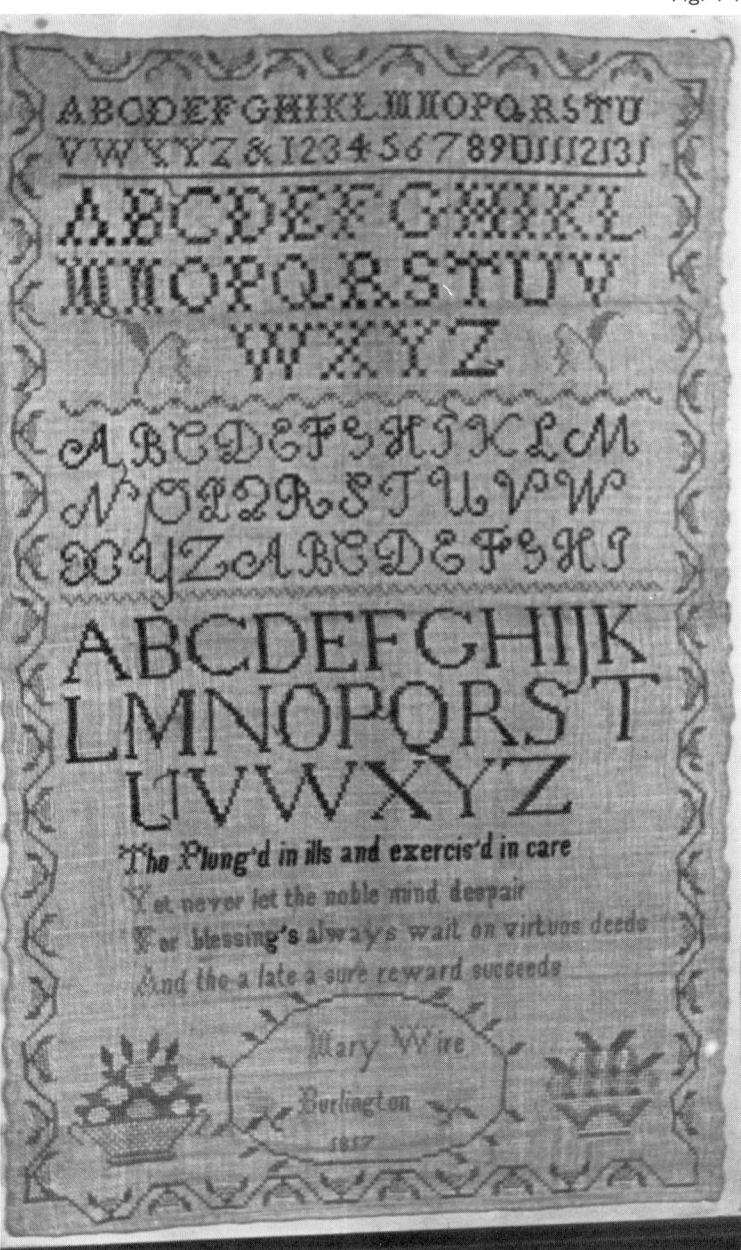

Fig. 72.

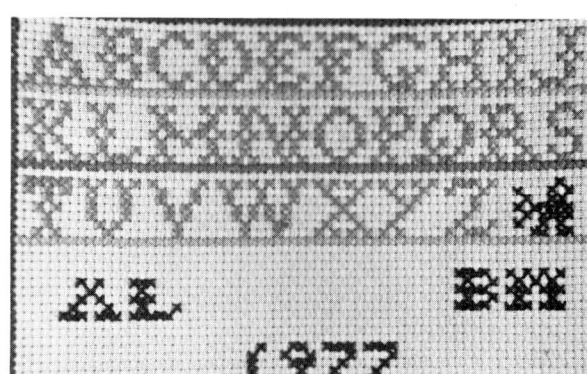

Fig. 73.

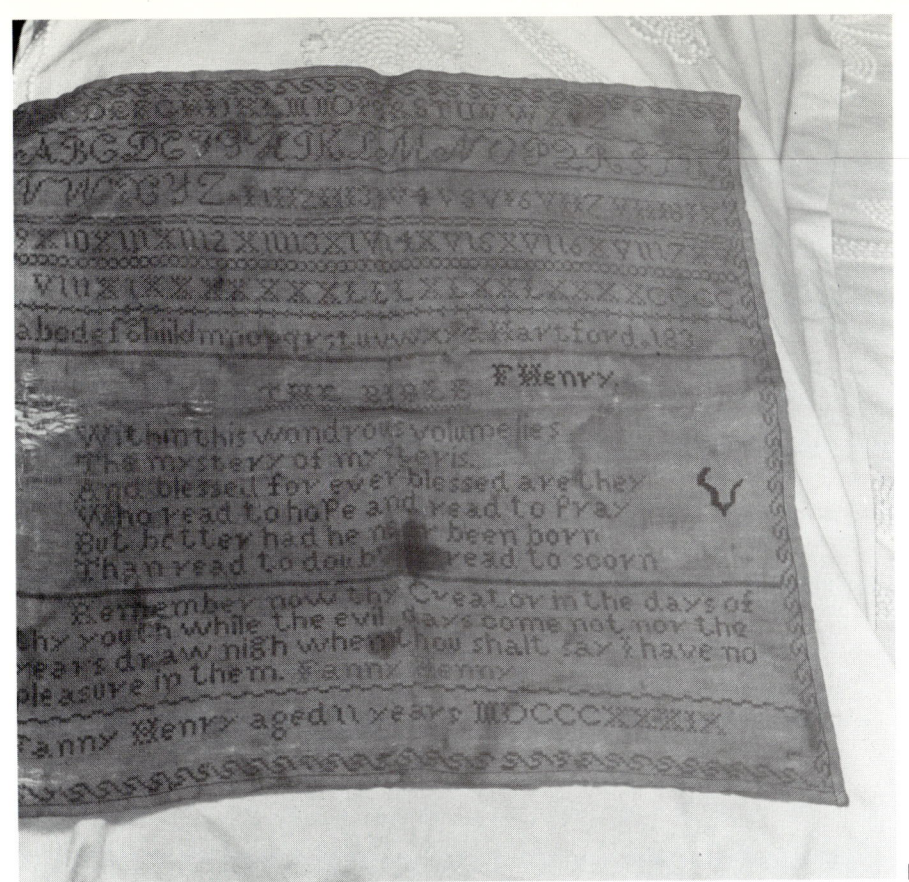

Fig. 75.

Fig. 76.

Sampler Texts and Verses

In the history of samplers, texts play an important part (Fig. 77). Commonly used were biblical quotations, The Lord's Prayer, The Ten Commandments, and verses on the themes of death, work, and religion. Some interesting examples are:

> Ann Stanfer is my name
> And England is my nation,
> Blackwall is my dwelling place,
> And Christ is my salvation.

This verse from an English sampler dated 1766 was also popular in America. By changing the person's name, the country, and the state or county, the verse remains the same. Here is an American version of the same verse from Burlington, New Jersey:

> Martha Kirby is my name
> Hanover is my station,
> Burlington is my dwelling place,
> And Christ is my salvation.

Fig. 77. Mary Shrove's sampler, dated July 25, 1807. Here is a front lawn with four bushes, a fence with a front gate, and a center motif is a basket overflowing with flowers. *Photo courtesy Burlington County Historical Society, Burlington, New Jersey; photo by Bruce Murphy*

One of the simplest verses used in samplers to indicate the name of the embroiderer was first found in 1675:

> Isabel Ercy is my name,
> And with my needle I wrought the same.

Also very common is:

> When this you see,
> Remember me.

And this verse appears in many American samplers:

> When I am dead and in my grave
> And all my bones be rotten,
> When this you see remember me
> Or I shall be forgotten.

Frequently found is this verse:

> Tho age must show life's best pursuits are vain
> And few the pleasures to be enjoyed,
> Yet may this work a pleasing proof remain,
> Of youth's gay period usefully employed.

A verse found in an American sampler in 1822 praises love:

> When two fond hearts as one unite,
> The yoke is easy and the burden light.

Parents are mentioned often in sampler verse:

> This I did to let you see
> What care my parents took of me.

Another mention of parents:

> Helen Price is my name,
> And in my youth I worked the same,
> And by my work you may plainly see,
> What care my parents took of me.

A popular verse in Europe and America:

> When I was young and in my prime,
> Here you may see how I spent my time.

A quaint verse was stitched in England by Frances Johnson in 1797:

> In reading this if any faults you see,
> Mend them yourself and find no fault in me.

On behalf of friendship, written in 1684 in a sampler bearing the names of Miles and Abigail Fleetwood:

> In prosperity friends are plenty
> In adversity not one in twenty.

Written in praise of learning, on a sampler completed in 1767:

> Adorn thyself with grace & truth
> And learning prize now in thy youth.

And in 1806:

> The youth with greatest talent born
> Is rough, while unrefined,
> Learning will every heart adorn
> And polish every mind.

Several verses found in the eighteenth and nineteenth centuries are suitable for contemporary samplers. One often seen reads:

> This needle work of mine can tell
> When I was young I learned well
> And by my elders I was taught
> Not to spend my time for naught.

And this verse:

> This to my friends when I am gone
> I leave for them to look upon
> Remember that I wrought the same
> For underneath you find my name.

From an American sampler completed in 1827:

> The canvas thus in colors laid
> Gives a just emblem of mankind
> Thus education good or bad
> Shows on the canvas of the mind.

Also from an American sampler, this one completed in 1794:

> For age and want save while you may
> No morning sun lasts a whole day.

Not all children enjoyed making a sampler. The charming text of ten-year-old Patty Polk's sampler (about 1800) reads:

> Patty Polk did this and she hated
> every stitch she did in it. She loves
> to read much more.

II desiqninq samplers: materials

Fabrics

Even-weave fabrics must be used when following a graphed project (Fig. 78). These fabrics allow you to make a perfect cross-stitch because the horizontal and vertical threads are woven at the same distance (even weave). Since a cross-stitch is worked over thread intersections, it will result in a perfectly square stitch.

Unlike needlepoint, a counted thread piece usually does not require you to stitch the entire background—taking less time to complete than a project done on canvas.

Even-Weave Linen. This material is ideal for counted thread embroidery. Its round threads are woven evenly. When working on linen, stitches usually cover two or three threads; each thread is counted when placing a stitch. For example, three horizontal threads and three vertical threads make a square cross-stitch. The counting can be done very quickly once the rhythm of stitching the designs is established.

Even-weave linen is usually imported from Switzerland, France, and Scandinavia. It is

Fig. 78. *Even-Weave Fabrics. Top left:* Aida cloth; *top right:* Hardanger cloth; *bottom left:* Even-weave linen (14 thread count); *bottom right:* Fine even-weave linen.

available in 14 to 36 thread counts per inch. Remember that the lower the thread count, the bulkier the fabric will be.

Linens in white, off-white, ecru, and other

pale or pastel colors are ideal for sampler projects.

Hardanger Cloth. This material is an even-weave cotton fabric, favored by needleworkers for many years. Each vertical and horizontal thread consists of two flat threads woven side by side and counting as one thread.

The most popular Hardanger cloth is 22 thread count (11 cross-stitches per inch).

Aida Cloth. Aida cloth is a basket-weave cotton fabric consisting of multistrand inter-locking flat threads. These are worked over as one unit horizontally and vertically. The holes on Aida cloth are very clearly defined, making stitching very easy.

On Aida and Hardanger cloth, stitches are always taken over one square of the fabric. On linen, stitches are taken over two or three threads vertically and horizontally.

Aida cloth is available in 11 or 14 threads per inch (11 is the coarser fabric and 14 the finer).

Other Fabrics. Coarse, flat-weaved fabrics such as *Monk's cloth* can be used for counted work. Follow the graph and count one stitch per square of fabric.

Gingham has been used by contemporary needleworkers for cross-stitch and some sampler projects. Follow the graph and make the crosses over each check. Gingham no larger than 7 or 8 squares per inch should be used.

Needlepoint canvas has also been used for sampler and cross-stitch projects. If you use a mono canvas 10-mesh to the inch, tapestry or persian yarn should be used. Continental stitch works well on this type of canvas. Penelope canvas has been used for sampler projects too. This double-thread canvas is woven with two threads per mesh. It can be worked in cross-stitch or continental stitch, and the double threads can be separated and tiny stitches can be worked between them.

When working on needlepoint canvas, the background can be left unfinished and only the motifs need to be stitched. A piece of fabric sewn to the back of the canvas before framing will create an interesting effect and the illusion of a finished background.

To cross-stitch on any fabric that is not even weave, such as muslin, medium-weight linen, linenlike cotton, or multipurpose fabrics, Penelope canvas is the solution. Charted designs can be cross-stitched on any fabric by working over a double-thread Penelope canvas basted to fabric (Fig. 79). Use the loosely woven Penelope canvas (not interlock) and any type of washable, colorfast fabric that does not shrink. Cut a piece of canvas larger than the area to be stitched. Baste to the fabric and place in an embroidery hoop. Work the crosses over the double mesh and through the fabric. Do not work the stitches through the small spaces of the canvas. When finished, remove the basting and the horizontal threads of the canvas one by one; then remove the vertical canvas threads (use tweezers if necessary), leaving the cross-stitched design on the fabric.

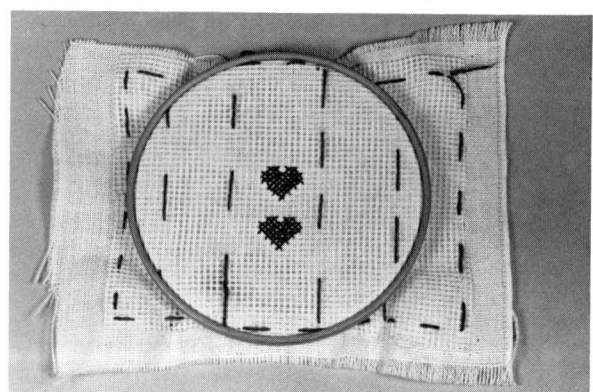

Fig. 79. Penelope canvas basted to fabric for cross-stitch embroidery.

Threads

Today we can find many varieties of embroidery thread available in hundreds of colors (Fig. 80).

Thread should be chosen according to the fabric selected for the project. The best way to find out which is most appropriate is by experimenting with different threads and number of strands. Salespersons in needlecraft stores may give you an idea of what is needed for a project; don't hesitate to ask.

Fig. 80. *Top:* Crewel wool; *Left to Right:* Rayon thread (2 skeins); six-strand cotton floss (2 skeins); Perle Cotton size 3 (2 skeins); Perle Cotton ball sizes 5 and 8.

Fig. 81. Cross-stitch pattern worked on heavyweight wool using tapestry yarn by Tove Simonsen.

Six-Strand Cotton Floss. It comes in 9-yard skeins, is available in hundreds of shades, and it is inexpensive. It can be split so you can work with the number of strands that looks best on the fabric. Has a slight sheen.

Heavy Cotton Threads. Matte-finished heavy cotton threads are 4-ply. Available in 11-yard skeins.

Danish Flower Thread. Single strand, twisted cotton floss, somewhat heavier than mercerized cotton.

Perle Cotton. Glossy, thick, twisted thread available in over 100 colors. It comes in several weights ranging from 1 (the thickest) to 8 (the finest). Most needleworkers prefer size 5 (in 53-yard balls) and size 8 (in 95-yard balls) for cross-stitching and embroidering.

Rayon Thread. Now available in most outlets that carry the six-strand floss. Rayon thread has a high sheen, comes in 7-yard skeins, and is made up of four strands that can be separated easily.

Crewel and Persian Wool. Can be used on wool even-weave fabrics or bulky fabrics (Fig. 81).

Experiment with the thread—use different numbers of strands, or double thickness of single-strand threads—until you are satisfied with the results. Usually, the bulkier or coarser the fabric is, the heavier thread you can use. The stitches you plan to use can also influence your decision. Metallic and other seldom used threads might lend an unusual touch to your project.

Needles

Even-weave fabrics are stitched using blunt needles. Tapestry needles have a blunt point that helps slip the thread easily between the fabric threads. They are available in sizes from 13 (the largest) to 26 (the smallest). However, sizes 24, 25, and 26 are preferred by needleworkers working on counted work projects.

Avoid sharp needles that can pierce the fabric. Crewel needles have sharp tips and large eyes; they can be used for working on fine linen, muslin, and other fabrics. These are available in sizes 1 (the largest) to 10 (the smallest).

An important point to remember: remove the needle from the fabric when you put your work away. Even the best needles will rust from moisture in the air. Place them in a safe place where you can find them easily. You can make a needle book by gluing fabric (such as felt) to a piece of vinyl or cardboard; fold it twice to make a three-part unit and secure with a safety pin, ribbon, or Velcro fasteners (Figs. 82 and 83).

Fig. 82.

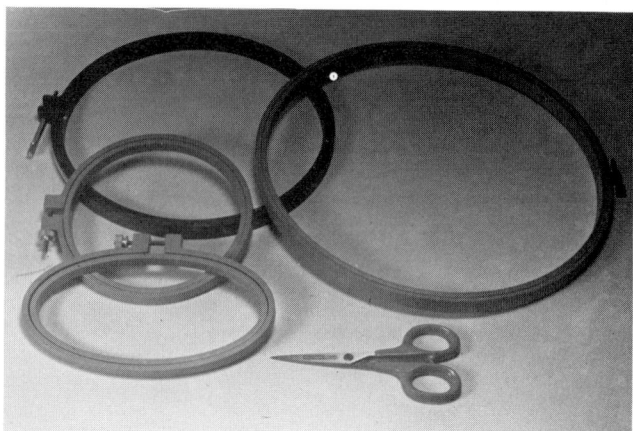

Fig. 84. Hoops are available in many sizes.

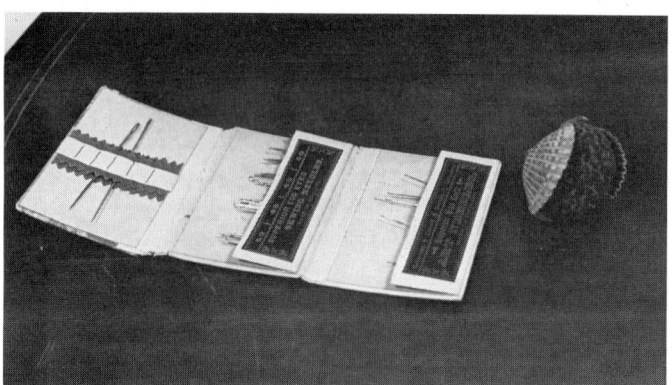

Fig. 83. Needle book and shell pincushion, circa 1800. *Courtesy Burlington Historical Society, Burlington, New Jersey*

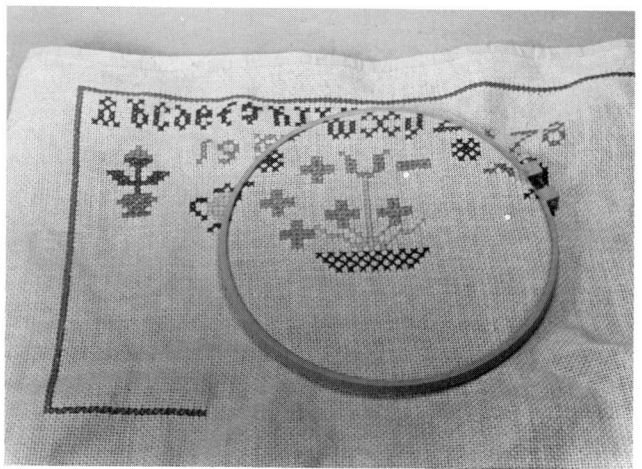

Fig. 85. Plastic Bates Hoop with Sure-Grip Lip is rustproof and durable.

Hoops

Traditionally, counted cross-stitch work has been done with the fabric held taut in a hoop. Most contemporary needleworkers still use a hoop or frame for this type of embroidery. Stitch tension will be more even, and holes between threads will be easier to find. Many embroidery stitches like satin stitch absolutely require the use of a hoop.

Hoops are available in many sizes and are made of wood, plastic, and metal with a screw or spring in the outer ring (Fig. 84). Experts prefer wooden hoops with the screw to control tension, although plastic hoops with a tight-grip lip are excellent (Fig. 85).

In addition to the hand-held hoop, there are hoops that can be clamped to table edges, hoops that stand on the floor, and hoops with a base on which the needleworker sits (Fig. 86). They are ideal for freeing both hands for embroidering.

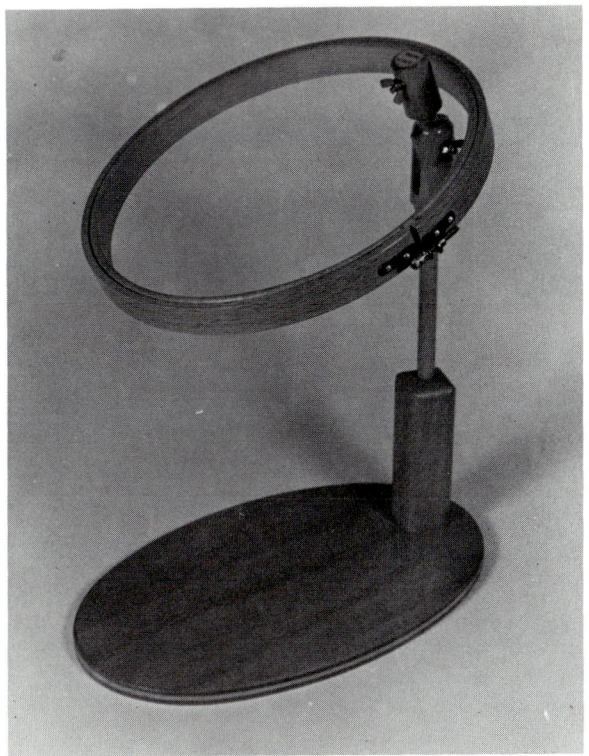

Fig. 86. Hoop by Kay & EE Corp.

work. They are available in most needlecraft stores.

Metal Boards. Metal boards with magnetic strips are ideal for holding a graph. The strips are placed under the row being worked, and you cannot lose your place while stitching (Fig. 87).

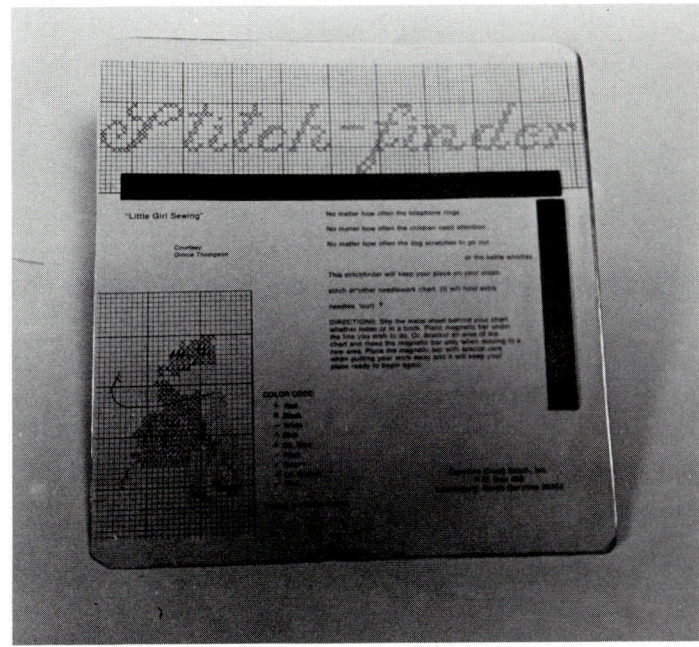

Fig. 87. A metal board with magnetic strips, such as Stitch-finder™, helps the needleworker to follow a cross-stitch graph.

The work should be removed from the hoop before it is put away.

Although cross-stitch is not damaged by fitting the hoop on it, you can place tissue over the finished work before fitting the hoop to protect it.

Other Materials

Scissors. Embroidery scissors, used for nothing else but embroidery, are essential. They are short (approximately 3 inches in length) and very sharp to snip stitches when a mistake is made. Keep scissors in a scissors case or use the folding type to prevent accidents.

Thimble. If you need a thimble when doing cross-stitch work, use one. If you feel uncomfortable with one, just put it away.

Magnifying glass. The magnifying glass that hangs from the neck has been found to be a great aid to those who are completing close

III PLANNING THE SAMPLER

Determining Size

Once you have chosen the fabric and prepared the chart for the project, the sampler's size should be determined.

To find the amount of fabric needed, count the number of cross-stitches per inch that your fabric requires. To do this, just work a one-inch line of cross-stitches. On the graph, count the number of squares the design occupies vertically. Divide the number of vertical squares by the number of stitches per inch; this equals the length of the sampler. Then divide the number of horizontal squares by the number of stitches per inch; this equals the width of the sampler. Add at least four inches of fabric all around for a margin, finishing and mounting.

Edges

To prevent edges from fraying, bind with masking tape folded over the edge (Fig. 88). Or make a narrow hem all around the sampler.

Basting

Stitch a basting guideline through the center

Fig. 88.

of the fabric from side to side and another from top to bottom. These lines might prove very convenient when working the sampler.

Stitching

Start at the top corner and work across. Then work the rest of the motifs down. Or work from the center stitch of the design out. Remove guidelines when the project is completed.

Finishing

If the sampler is very clean, just place it on a clean towel on the ironing board, right side down. Iron it using a dry iron; dampen the sampler with a wet cloth or spray bottle.

If the sampler needs to be washed, wash it gently with a cold water wash or mild soap solution. Rinse well but do not wring. Roll it on a thick towel several times to remove excess water. Then spread the sampler flat, right side down, and iron while still damp.

Mounting and Framing

Samplers can be stretched and mounted on a cardboard backing and framed for display. They should always be framed under glass to protect the finished piece from dust.

Framing your sampler for display can be done two ways. The first and easiest is to have it done by a professional frame shop. It is more expensive, but you are assured a perfect job when the framer does it.

The second way is to do it yourself. Ready-made frames can sometimes be used to avoid the expense of having a frame especially made for the sampler.

The first step in stretching or mounting your sampler is to determine the size of the cardboard backing needed. A ½-inch or wider

border should be left around all sides of the sampler after it has been stretched. First measure the sampler and then add 1 inch to the length and width. This will give you a ½-inch border around the sampler. Then cut a piece of 2-ply illustration board of that size (Fig. 89).

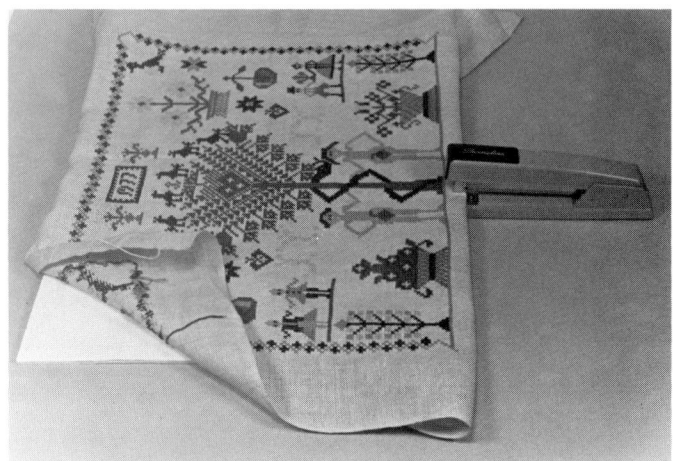

Fig. 90.

Next center your sampler on the board, fold under one edge, and staple along the edge. Do the same for the opposite edge, pulling the sampler taut as you staple. Turn the sampler and staple once in each of the remaining two sides (Fig. 90). The sampler can now be stapled securely around the entire piece of board. Try to keep the borders straight when stapling.

After the sampler has been attached to the board, fold the corners neatly under in the back, and staple (Fig. 91).

Your mounted sampler should look something like this when finished (Fig. 92). The sampler is then placed in the frame. Cover the back of the frame with a piece of brown wrapping paper and tape around the edges of it with package sealing tape. This will protect the sampler from any type of airborne pollutants that might damage it.

Fig. 89.

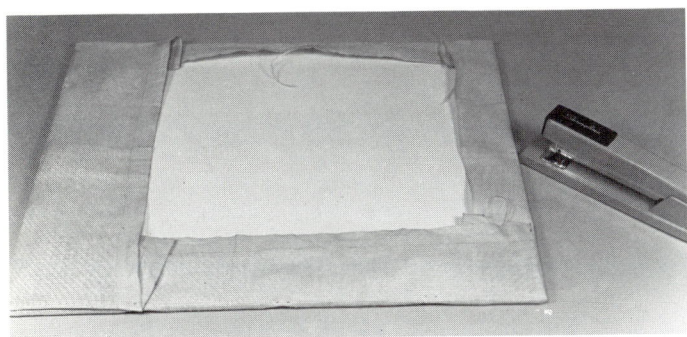

Fig. 91.

Fig. 92.

Hints

The following hints might help you through the different stages of designing your sampler:
• When doing cross-stitch embroidery always have the bottom half of *all* crosses in one direction, and *all* top half that crosses them in the other direction.
• Use a small hoop such as 4-, 5-, or 6-inch plastic or wood.
• Keep thread skeins tied to a yarn card or braid them.
• Get ideas for designing your own sampler from samplers in museums, historical societies, and books. Adapt any motifs by charting on graph paper. It is easier than you think.
• Pull the fabric taut as you work on the hoop.
• Cut thread strands 18 to 20 inches long; if longer the thread will tangle.
• When a mistake is made, don't attempt to "unembroider" with the needle. It is better to cut the stitches carefully with embroidery scissors and start that section again.
• Finish a motif by carefully weaving the thread through completed rows.

IV stitches

The most important stitch found in samplers is the cross-stitch. Two methods are used when working cross-stitch. One is to make a complete cross from two diagonal stitches, the first stitch from lower right to upper left; the second stitch crosses it from lower left to upper right. Each cross-stitch is completed before going to the next.

The other method is to stitch a line of half cross-stitches and complete with the other half cross on the return to the initial point.

Use whichever method you feel most comfortable with, but make sure that the lower half cross is always in the same direction and the upper half cross is always slanted in the same direction.

Other stitches to be used in sampler projects, especially if there is embroidery to be worked, are: *stem stitch* for fillings, stems of flowers, outlines; *satin stitch* for filling leaves, petals, animal bodies; *split stitch* for lines and fillings; *seeding stitch* for light or heavy fillings (place the stitches closer for heavier fillings, apart for lighter); *French knot* for dots, lines,

fillings, details; *buttonhole stitches* are ideal for edges and outlines; *chain stitches* for

Fig. 93. CROSS

backgrounds and outlines; *arrowhead stitch* is used for open fillings and as a single decorative line; *backstitch* is used for lines, stems, borders, and outlines.

As you become more familiar with the stitches, you will find different uses for them.

Fig. 94. HERRINGBONE   Fig. 95. SATIN   Fig. 96. STEM

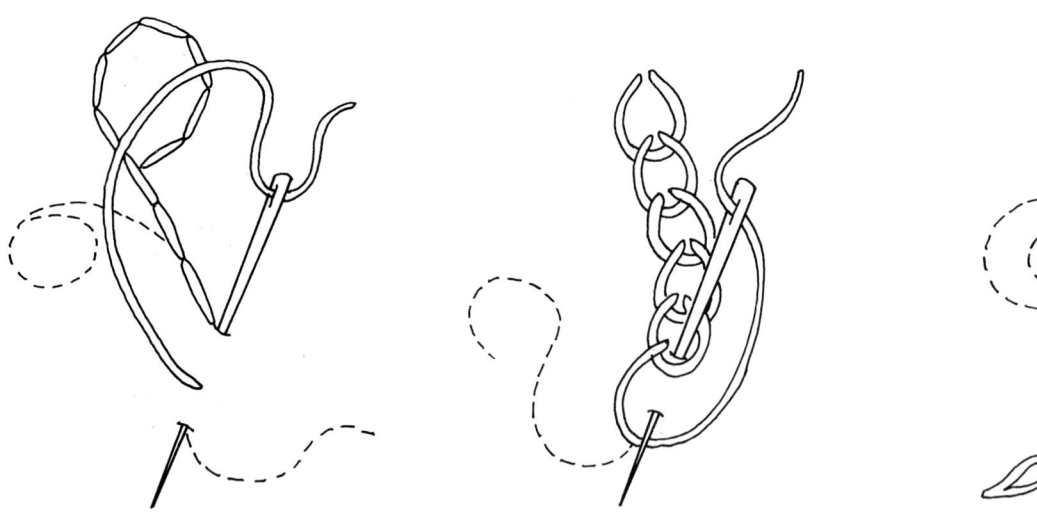

Fig. 97. BACK   Fig. 98. CHAIN   Fig. 99. SPLIT

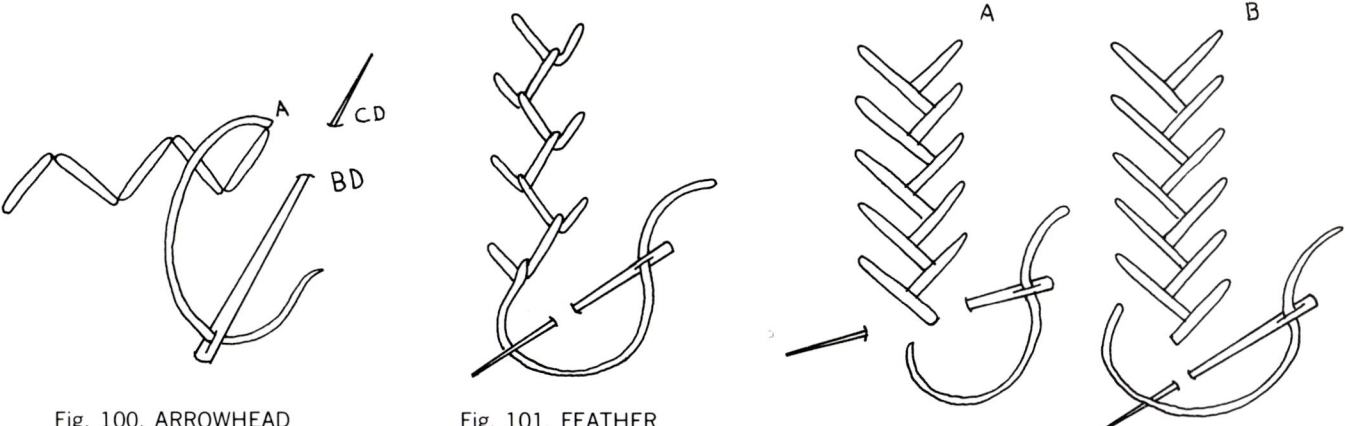

Fig. 100. ARROWHEAD

Fig. 101. FEATHER

Fig. 102. FISHBONE

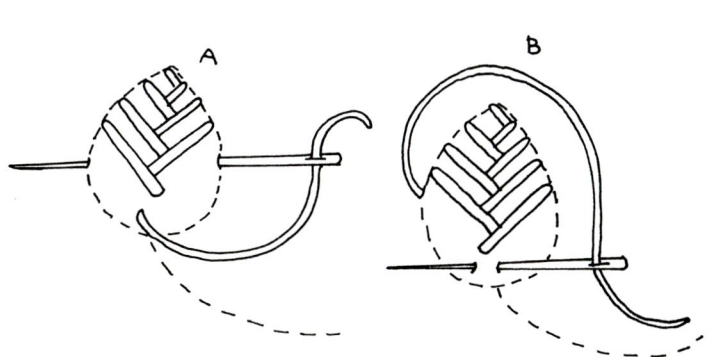

Fig. 103. FILLING WITH FISHBONE

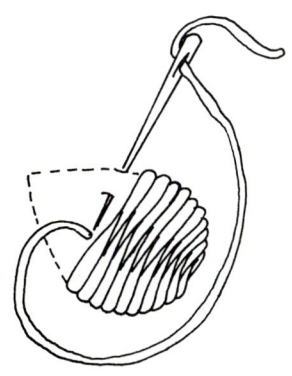

Fig. 104. FLAT

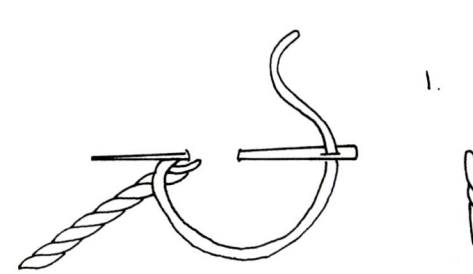

Fig. 105. HEM

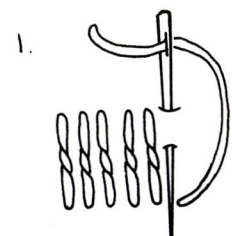

Fig. 106. ROUMANIAN

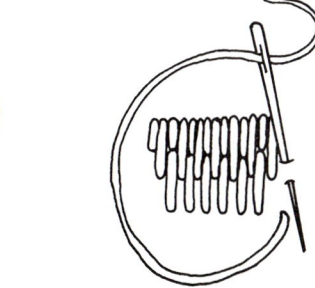

Fig. 107. BRICK

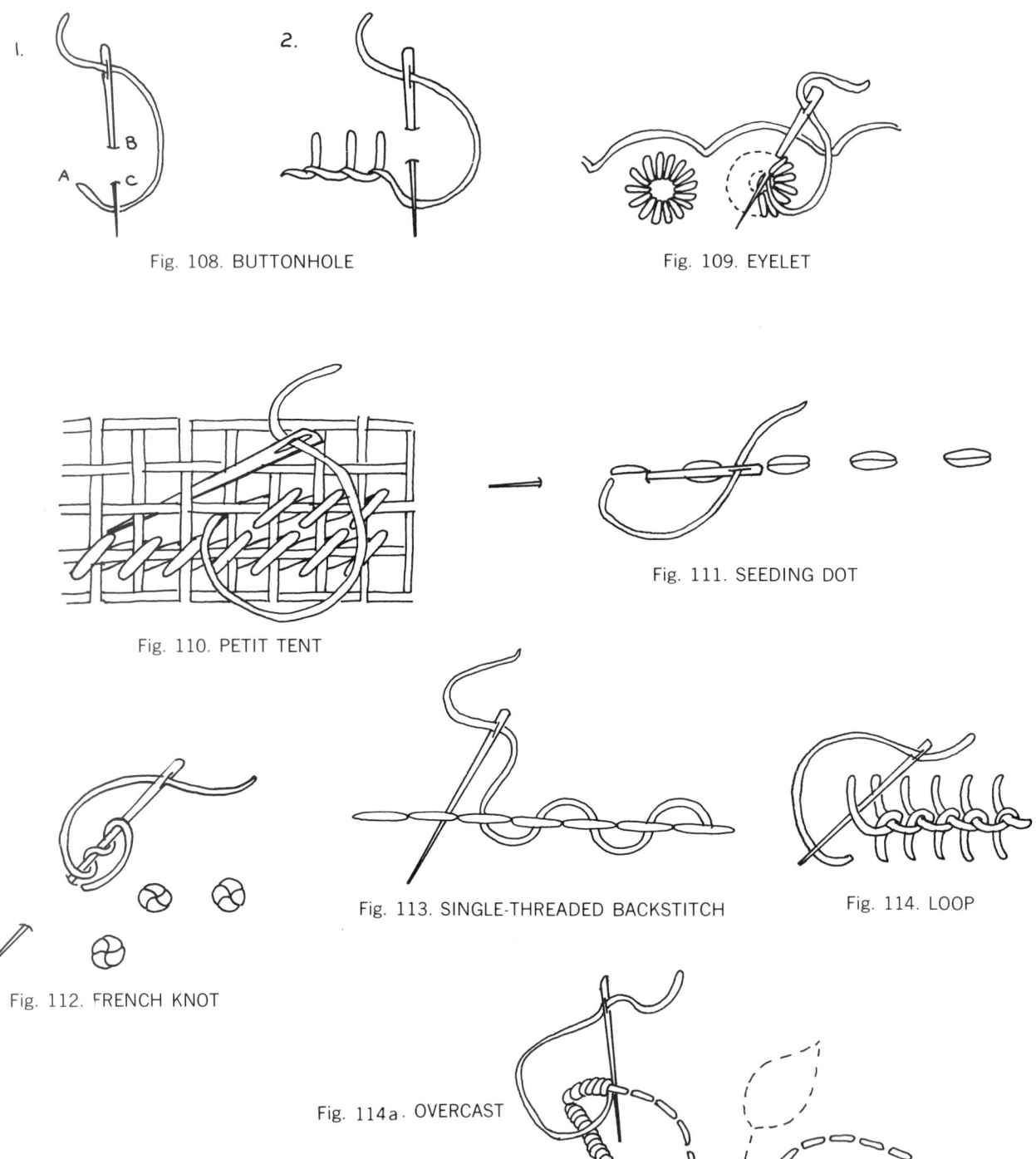

Fig. 108. BUTTONHOLE

Fig. 109. EYELET

Fig. 110. PETIT TENT

Fig. 111. SEEDING DOT

Fig. 112. FRENCH KNOT

Fig. 113. SINGLE-THREADED BACKSTITCH

Fig. 114. LOOP

Fig. 114a. OVERCAST

V 15 SAMPLER PROJECTS

Fig. 115. Adam and Eve Sampler
By Judy Thompson

Fig. 116. Detail

1. Adam and Eve Sampler
(by Judy Thompson)

The Adam and Eve motif was first used in American samplers during the eighteenth century. In this sampler Adam and Eve stand on each side of the serpent climbing a stylized Dutch tree of life. The spaces around the tree are filled in with various baskets of flowers, fruits, birds, and people. All stitches in this sampler are cross-stitches (Figs. 115 and 116).

Fig. 115. ADAM AND EVE SAMPLER

ORANGE

BLACK

YELLOW

BURGUNDY

GREEN

BROWN

SAND

LIGHT BLUE

Fig. 117. Pennsylvania German Compendium Sampler
By Ana G. Lopo

2. Pennsylvania German Compendium Sampler
(by Ana G. Lopo)

A compendium sampler is composed of different scattered motifs. Pennsylvania German samplers, unlike other American samplers, remained basically the same in design through the years. The entire sampler is done in cross-stitch (Figs. 117 and 118).

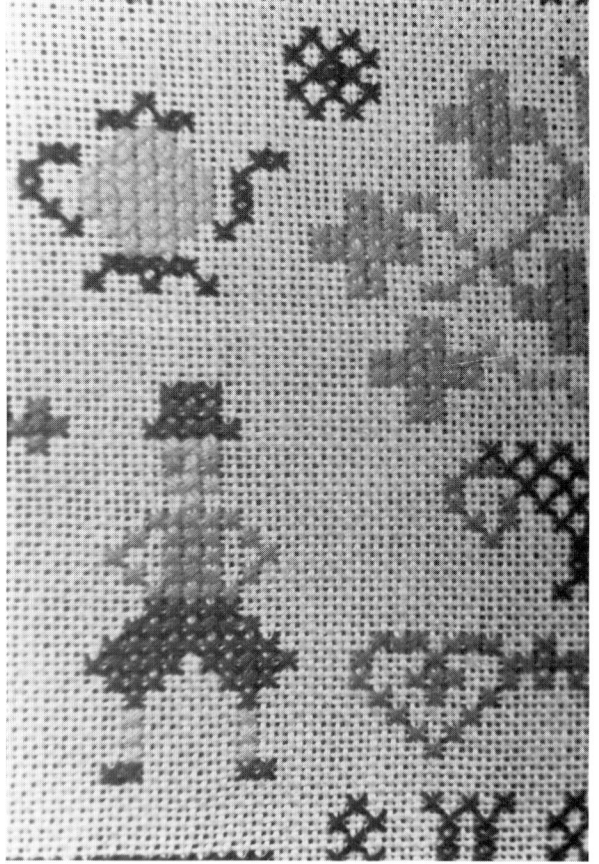

Fig. 118. Detail

Fig. 117. PENNSYLVANIA GERMAN COMPENDIUM SAMPLER

OCHER		
NAVY		
GREEN		
ROSE		
BURGUNDY		
PINK		
ORANGE		
BLUE		
LIGHT GREEN		
LIGHT BLUE		
BROWN		
YELLOW		

Fig. 119. BLACK SHEEP SAMPLER

GREEN

BROWN

BLUE

FLESH

BLACK

KELLY GREEN

BURGUNDY

YELLOW

PURPLE

LIGHT BLUE

DARK GREEN

SAND

DARK BROWN

OCHER

Fig. 119. Black Sheep Sampler
By Barbara Egner

3. Black Sheep Sampler
(by Barbara Egner)

This sampler contains many of the characteristic design elements used first at the Mary Balch Academy in Providence, Rhode Island, between 1785 and 1800. Sheep, shepherds, and angels were often used in eighteenth-century sampler designs. All motifs are done in cross-stitch (Figs. 119 and 120).

Fig. 120. Detail

52

Fig. 121. Alphabet Sampler
By Bruce W. Murphy

Fig. 122. Detail

4. Alphabet Sampler
(by Bruce W. Murphy)

In early American schools, needlework was part of the curriculum. Samplers from dame schools (by young girls) were usually just alphabets. The alphabet sampler was completed before a more complicated sampler was attempted. The wool fabric used for this sampler has been dyed dark green. Samplers stitched on a dark green fabric using light colors were found only in the Philadelphia area. The alphabets are done in cross-stitch and the red border is done in satin stitch (Figs. 121 and 122).

Fig. 121. ALPHABET SAMPLER

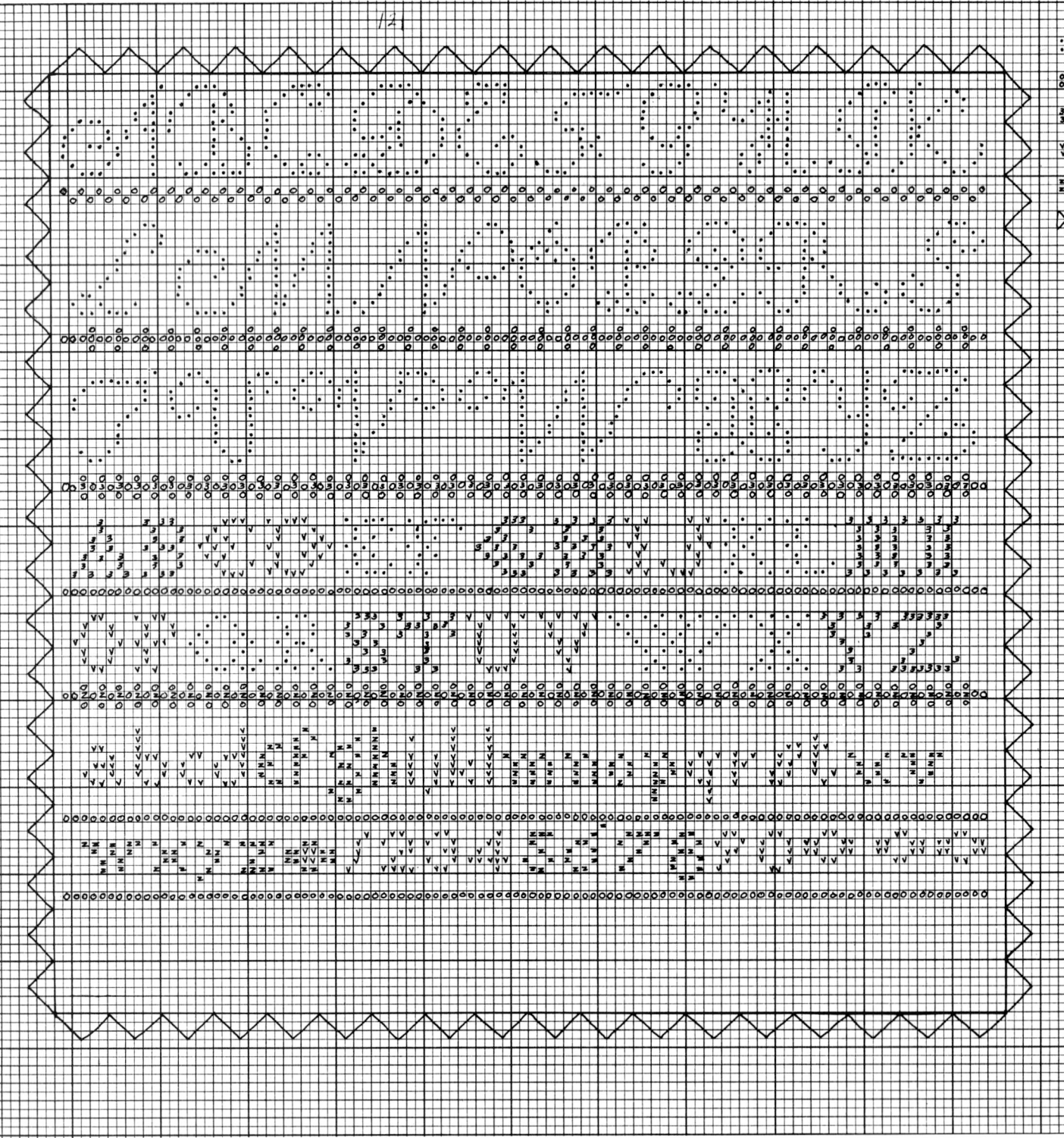

YELLOW
WHITE
RED
OCHER
BLUE
CARDINAL

Fig. 123. Trenton Sampler
By Bruce W. Murphy

5. Trenton Sampler
(by Bruce W. Murphy)

This sampler is composed of cross-stitched and embroidered designs. The embroidered basket of flowers is characteristic of samplers found in the Philadelphia and Trenton, New Jersey, areas. A wide cross-stitched flower border frames each side of the flower basket and alphabets. Across the top is a house, or the architectural element, often seen in samplers. The flowers, animals, and leaves are done in satin stitch. The stems and basket outline are done in stem stitch (Figs. 123 and 124).

Fig. 124. Detail

Fig. 123. TRENTON SAMPLER

GREEN

BURGUN

YELLOW

BURNT
SIENNA

BLUE

PINK

LIGHT
GREEN

SAND

N-NAVY

P-PINK

R-ROSE

BS-BUR
SIENNA

G-GREE

LG-LIGH
GREEN

BG-BLU
GREEN

DG-DAR
GREEN

Y-YELLO

C-CORA

GO-GOL

BU-
BURGU

B-BROW

DR-DAR
RED

Fig. 125. Pennsylvania Dutch Heart Sampler
By Ana G. Lopo

Fig. 126. Detail

6. Pennsylvania Dutch Heart Sampler
(by Ana G. Lopo)

Pennsylvania Dutch samplers are composed of motifs that are angular and rather stiff. The more realistic treatment of designs that appear in other American samplers of the nineteenth century are not seen in Pennsylvania Dutch samplers. Borders were seldom used, while peacocks and hearts appeared in many samplers. All stitches in this piece are cross-stitches (Figs. 125 and 126).

Fig. 125. PENNSYLVANIA DUTCH HEART SAMPLER

LIGHT BLUE	
NAVY	
LIGHT PINK	
PINK	
RED ORANGE	
BLUE	
LIGHT GREEN	
BLUE GREEN	

Fig. 127. Ana's Sampler
By Ana G. Lopo

7. Ana's Sampler
(by Ana G. Lopo)

A three-sided border is used in this sampler; this was the predecessor of the four-sided border. It is a good sampler for a beginner. Done on Aida cloth, a very even cross-stitch can be achieved. This sampler is also given as a complete iron-on transfer in the transfer section of the book. It is done completely in cross-stitches (Figs. 127 and 128).

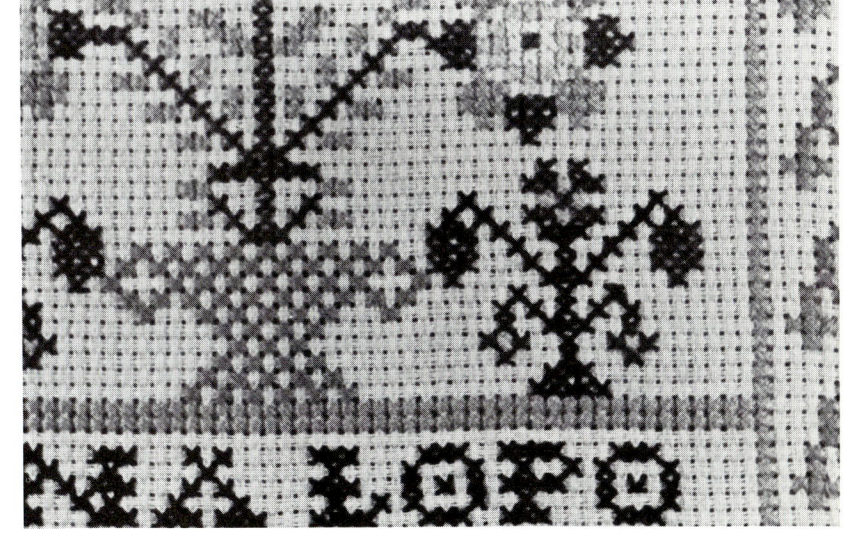

Fig. 127. ANA'S SAMPLER

NAVY

LIGHT GREEN

GOLDEN BROWN

GOLD

BLUE

PINK

GREEN

RED

DARK GREEN

WHITE

Fig. 129. Peacock Sampler
By Ana G. Lopo

8. Peacock Sampler
(by Ana G. Lopo)

The peacocks in this sampler are typical motifs often seen in Dutch samplers. This sampler is a complete iron-on transfer in the transfer section of this book. Only cross-stitches are used in this sampler (Figs. 129 and 130).

Fig. 130. Detail

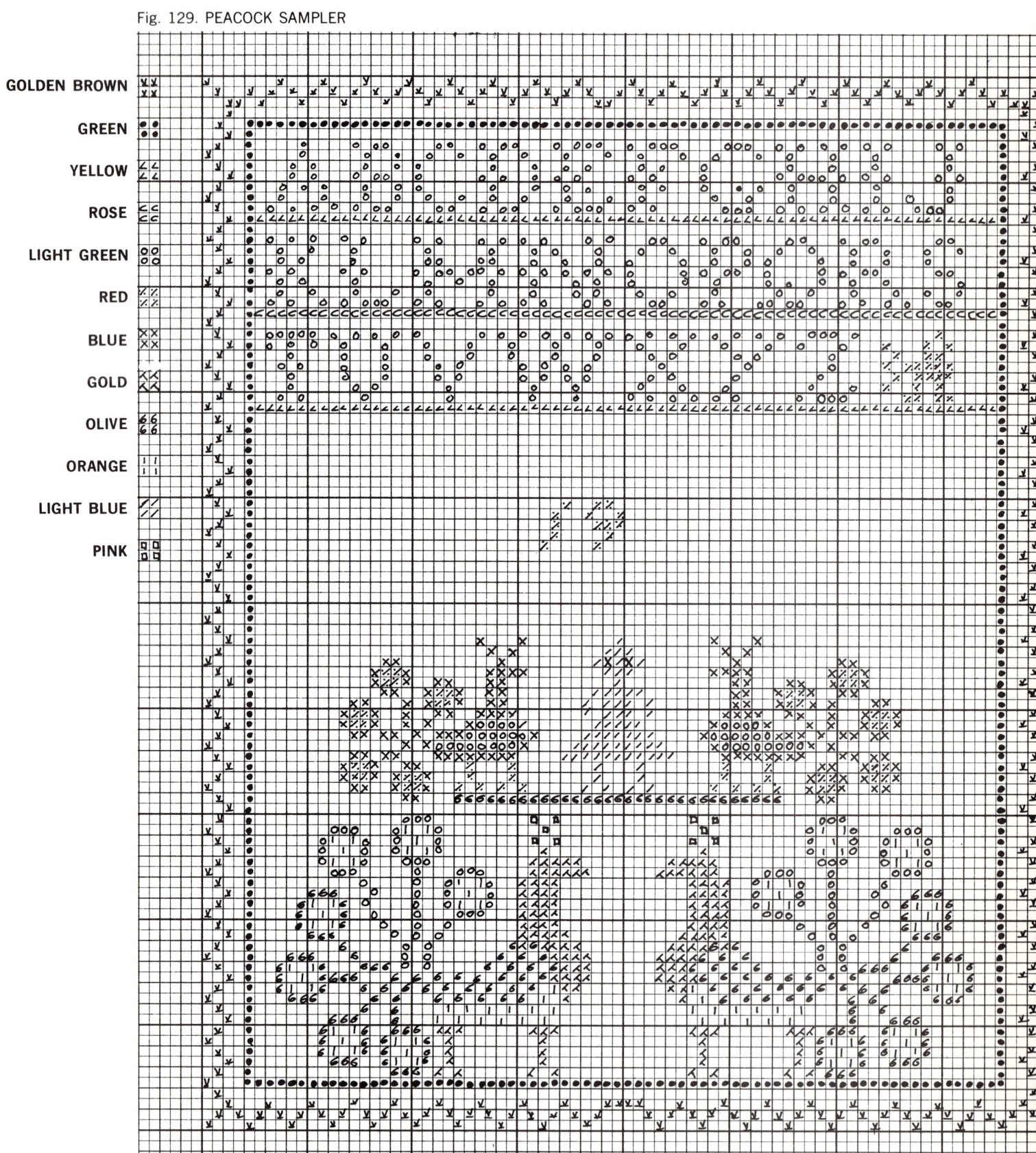

Fig. 129. PEACOCK SAMPLER

GOLDEN BROWN

GREEN

YELLOW

ROSE

LIGHT GREEN

RED

BLUE

GOLD

OLIVE

ORANGE

LIGHT BLUE

PINK

Fig. 131. Angels and Alphabet Sampler
By Bruce W. Murphy

9. Angels and Alphabet Sampler
(by Bruce W. Murphy)

Two very stylized angels flank a basket of flowers in this sampler. Alongside the alphabet is an embroidered border that became popular at the beginning of the nineteenth century. See the transfer section for this complete sampler design. The flower border is done in stem stitch for the stems and satin stitch for the flowers and leaves (Figs. 131 and 132).

Fig. 132. Detail

Fig. 131. ANGELS AND ALPHABET SAMPLER

		BLUE		RED ORANGE		SAND		BLACK		RED		LIGHT GREEN		GREEN		G-GREEN		R-RED

Fig. 133. Long Dutch Sampler
By Bruce W. Murphy

10. Long Dutch Sampler
(by Bruce W. Murphy)

An unusual sampler with its "border within a border" design. It is also horizontal instead of the usual vertical or square design. Included in its design are many of the motifs common to Dutch samplers. This sampler is done in cross-stitches (Figs. 133 and 134).

Fig. 134. Detail

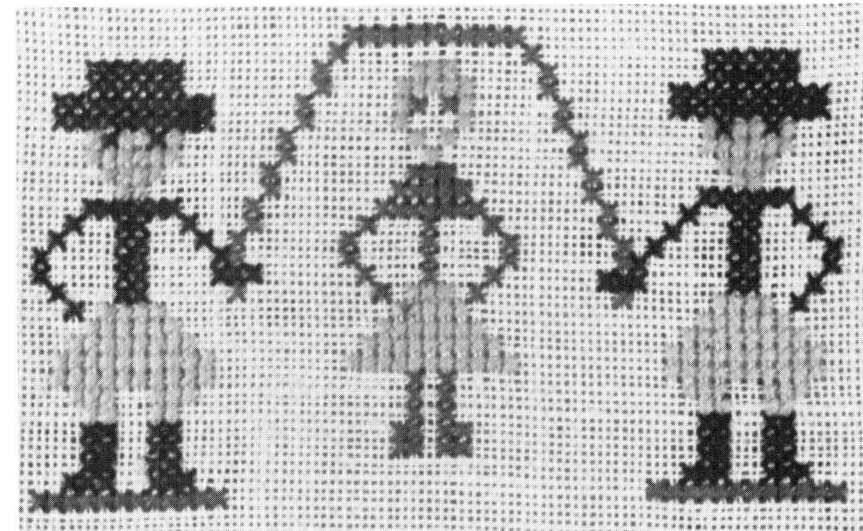

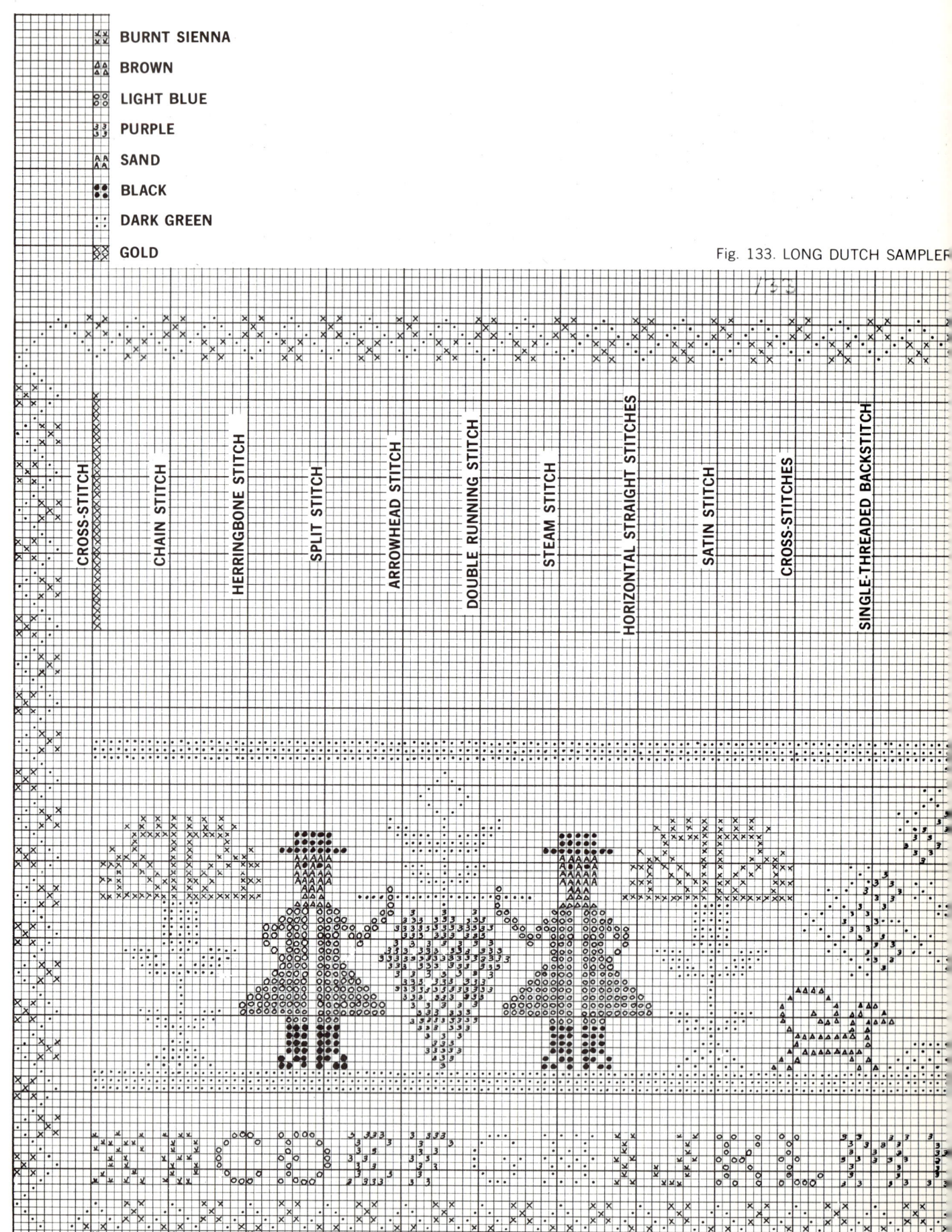

Fig. 133. LONG DUTCH SAMPLER

Legend:
- BURNT SIENNA
- BROWN
- LIGHT BLUE
- PURPLE
- SAND
- BLACK
- DARK GREEN
- GOLD

CROSS-STITCH

CHAIN STITCH

HERRINGBONE STITCH

SPLIT STITCH

ARROWHEAD STITCH

DOUBLE RUNNING STITCH

STEAM STITCH

HORIZONTAL STRAIGHT STITCHES

SATIN STITCH

CROSS-STITCHES

SINGLE-THREADED BACKSTITCH

Fig. 135. Dutch Sampler
By Bruce W. Murphy

11. Dutch Sampler
(by Bruce W. Murphy)

A typically Dutch border with flowers frames the initials of the makers of this sampler. This sampler is a complete iron-on transfer in the transfer section of the book. The entire sampler is done in cross-stitch (Fig. 135).

Fig. 135. DUTCH SAMPLER

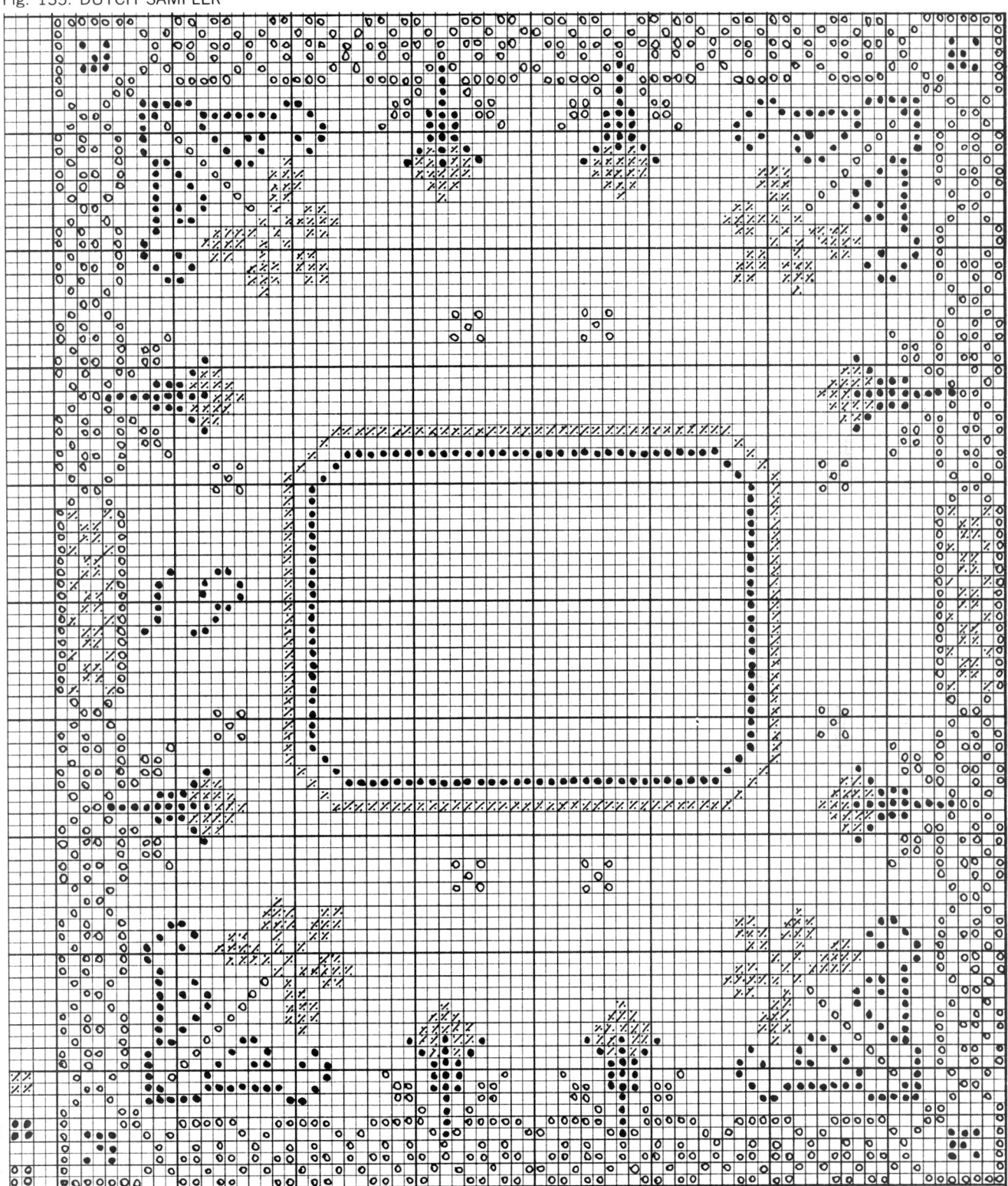

BURNT SIENNA

DARK GREEN

YELLOW

69

Fig. 136. EMBROIDERED AND PAINTED SAMPLER

DG-DARK GREEN

G-GREEN

LG-LIGHT GREEN

GO-GOLD

RB-RED BROWN

P-PINK

BL-BLUE

B-BLACK

LB-LIGHT BROWN

CP-CORAL PINK

W-WHITE

71

Fig. 136. Embroidered and Painted Sampler
By Bruce W. Murphy

Fig. 137. Detail

12. Embroidered and Painted Sampler
(by Bruce W. Murphy)

All elements of this sampler are done in various embroidery stitches; stem and satin stitch are used exclusively. The alphabet appears on a blue background that has been painted with fabric paint. A primitive charm makes up for any lack of accuracy in perspective and detail. This design is given as a complete iron-on sampler in the transfer section of this book. All flower stems are done in a stem stitch, as is the tree and alphabet. The rest of the sampler is done in a satin stitch (Figs. 136 and 137).

72

Fig. 138. Country House Sampler
By Bruce W. Murphy

Fig. 139. Detail

13. Country House Sampler
(by Bruce W. Murphy)

American sampler motifs were often things that were part of everyday life, transformed into cross-stitched designs. Houses were one of the most common motifs used, since life was centered around the home. Use only cross-stitches for this sampler (Figs. 138 and 139).

Fig. 138. COUNTRY HOUSE SAMPLER

BROWN

DARK GREEN

LIGHT GREEN

RED

BURGUNDY

NAVY

SAND

BLACK

PINK

YELLOW GOLD

ROSE

BLUE

LIGHT BLUE

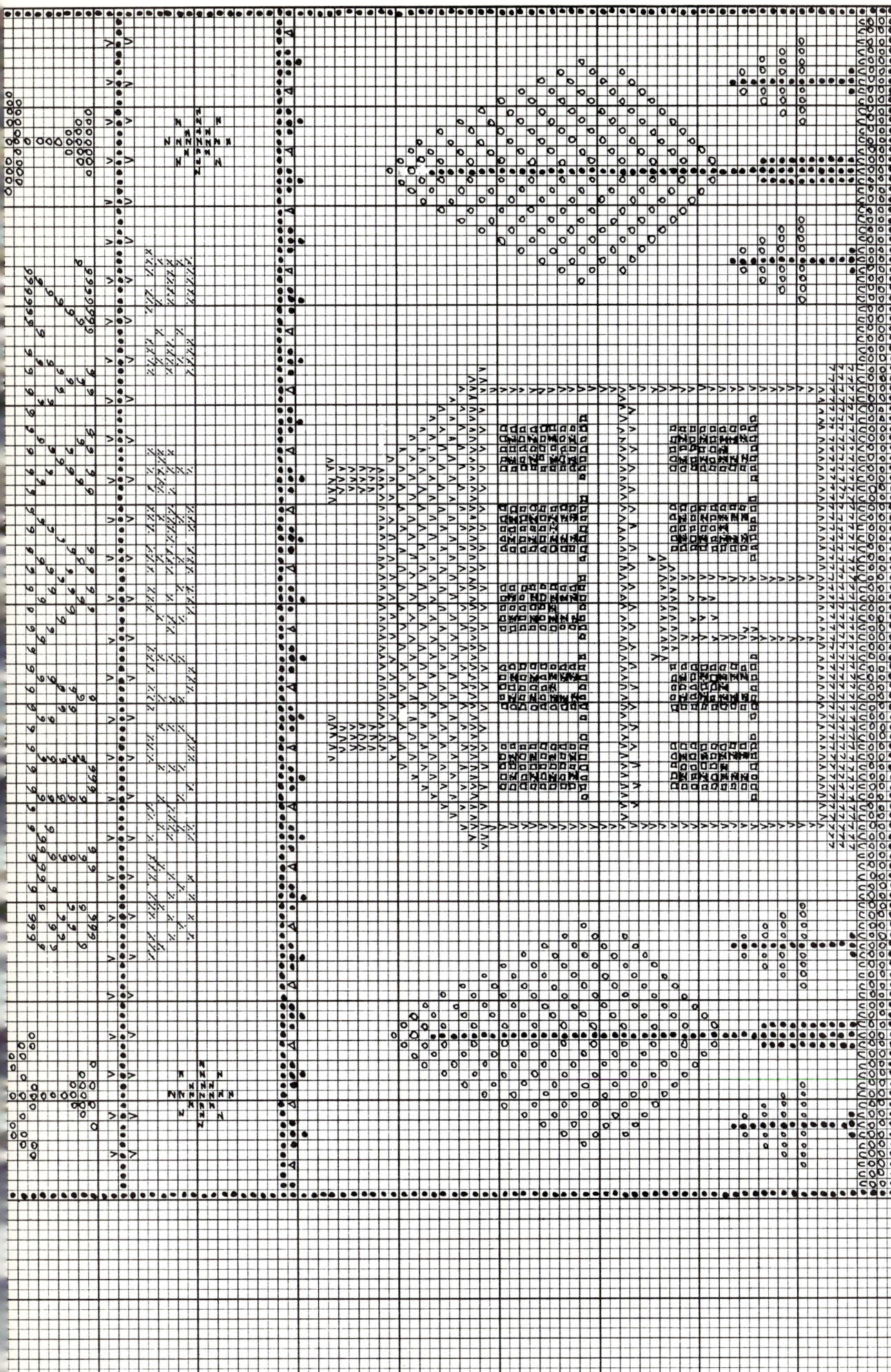

Fig. 140. FARM SAMPLER

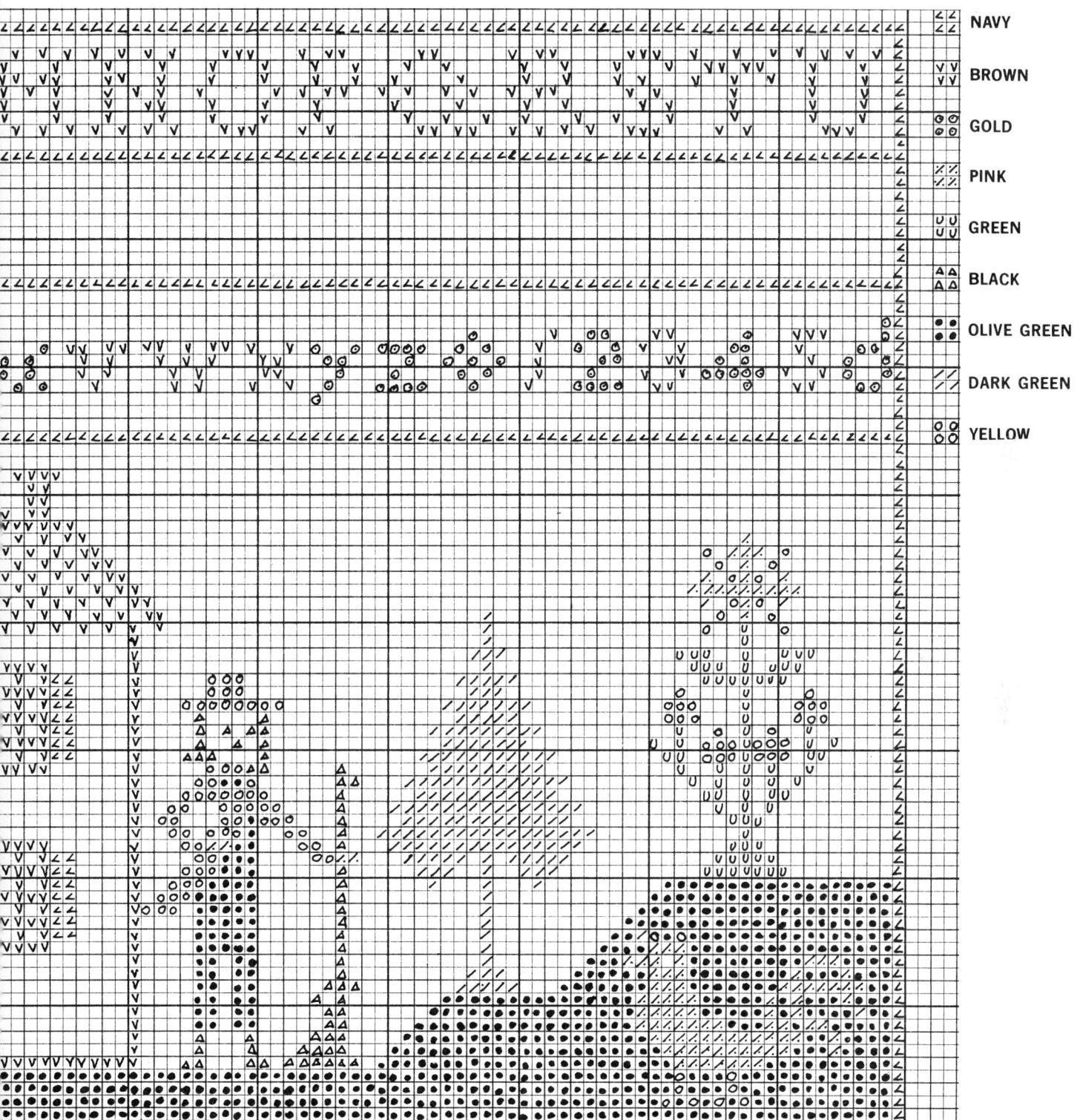

NAVY

BROWN

GOLD

PINK

GREEN

BLACK

OLIVE GREEN

DARK GREEN

YELLOW

77

Fig. 140. Farm Sampler
By Bruce W. Murphy

Fig. 141. Detail

14. Farm Sampler
(by Bruce W. Murphy)

An early American farm is stitched in this sampler. The use of a blue Aida cloth creates the illusion of a sky behind the scene. All designs in this sampler are composed of cross-stitches (Figs. 140 and 141).

Fig. 142. Nineteenth-Century American Sampler
By Bruce W. Murphy

15. Nineteenth-Century American Sampler (by Bruce W. Murphy)

This large sampler is quite typical of those popular in the nineteenth century in America. Given as a full size iron-on transfer, it will offer its maker many hours of stitching pleasure. This sampler is composed of three stitches: cross-stitch, stem stitch, and satin stitch (Figs. 142 and 143).

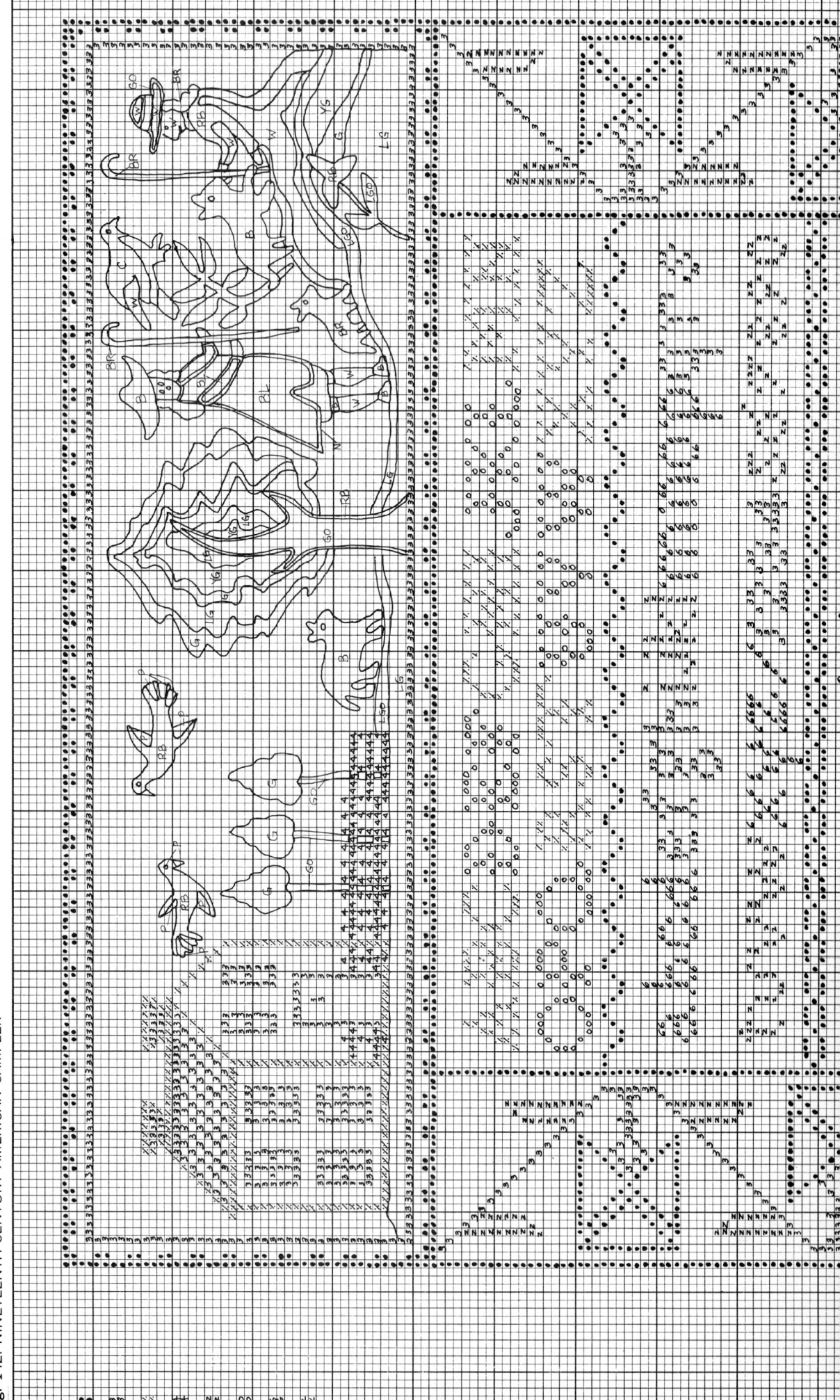

Fig. 142. NINETEENTH-CENTURY AMERICAN SAMPLER

80

81

VI TRANSFERRING designs

Using the Design Graphs

Designs for counted work like cross-stitch and also needlepoint are always charted. These charts or graphs simply indicate the number of stitches per line required to complete a motif. One square on the graph equals one cross-stitch (or one square of the fabric).

To start embroidering, choose a top corner or row of the design or motif. As you push your needle up a hole on the fabric, leave approximately 1 inch of thread on the wrong side of the fabric, and hold with your finger. With the next few stitches, the thread will be secured, as you work over it.

After one row is completed, do the next, always following the squares on the graph. If color-coded, each square on the graph will be filled with a different code (z, x, /, =, etc.). Each different code means a different color should be used for all stitches marked.

You can enlarge a design by stitching it on an even-weave fabric with a low thread count. The opposite is true for reducing a design on even weave.

Using the Iron-on Transfers

Types of Fabrics Suitable for Use. A smooth cotton, linen, or canvas type of fabric is best suited for use with transfer designs. Always test the fabric you have chosen with the test sample provided before you try to transfer an entire design. This will save you time and will enable you to get the most use from the transfers. A textured fabric should never be used, nor should glazed or resin-finished fabrics.

Fabric Colors. White, off-white, beige, or light-colored fabrics are best suited for use with transfer designs. Dark colors or a blue color like that of the transfer ink will not work. The transfer design should read clear and be easy to follow. Always try a test sample first.

Heat Settings for Iron. For a complete transfer, use a hot, dry iron set at a wool setting. No scorching should occur at this setting. Scorching can occur at a cotton setting. To prevent this, place a piece of tissue paper or light fabric between the iron and the transfer.

Reusing the Transfers. The transfer designs

can be used for a second time, and sometimes for a third. To see how the design will reproduce the second time, use a test sample that has already been used once before. Iron test sample for 10 seconds. If the transfer is not clear, iron for another 5 to 10 seconds, or until it can be easily seen. Make a note of how many seconds it takes for this second transfer to occur. Use this time for the sampler transfer.

How to Transfer Designs to Fabric. Experiment with a test sample first. Smooth the fabric out on the ironing board, or iron first to remove any wrinkles that might cause a distortion in the transfer. The test sample is then placed *printed side face down* onto the fabric. The iron is then placed on top of the test sample and fabric for 10 to 15 seconds. Do not move the iron during this time. Count the seconds on a watch and then lift the iron straight up. Next lift up a corner of the test sample to see if the transfer is clear. If not visible, more time will be needed.

Transferring Complete Sampler Designs. Pin the sampler transfer to the fabric (with the transfer's darkest side down). Follow the same procedure you used for the test sample: place the iron 10 to 15 seconds on a corner section of the sampler. Carefully lift the iron and proceed to the nearest section. Do not move the iron around or it will blur the motifs. Do this section by section, until the entire sampler has been transferred.

Using the Transfer Designs Permanently. If you like a motif or sampler that is iron-on, you can use it several times as a transfer. However, after a few times the ink is no longer transferable. You can make that motif or sampler a permanent part of your cross-stitch and embroidery designs by copying the design square by square on heavy graph paper.

bibliography

Bolton, Ethel, and Coe, Eva. *American Samplers*. New York: Dover Publications, 1973.

Grow, Judith K., and McGrail, Elizabeth C. *Creating Historic Samplers*. Princeton, N.J.: Pyne Press, 1974.

Huish, Mark. *Tapestry Embroideries*. New York: Dover Publications, 1938.

Lopo, Ana G., and Murphy, Bruce W. *The Needlecraft Manual*. New York: Drake Publishers, 1977.

Neuwburg, Alberta. *Embroidery Motifs from Dutch Samplers*. New York: Charles Scribner's Sons, 1974.

Schiffer, Margaret B. *Historical Needlework of Pennsylvania*. New York, 1968.

Story of Samplers, The. Philadelphia Museum of Art, 1971.

SOURCES of supply

You can write the following manufacturers for information. They can give you the names and addresses of dealers in your area who carry their products, or sell to you by mail.

AMARO & SONS
3641 Fireway Drive
San Diego, California 92111

(Complete line of stretchers, stands, hoops, and footstools.)

BOUTIQUE MARGOT
25 West 54th Street
New York, New York 10019
(212) 246-7244

(Complete line of imported threads, even-weave fabrics, canvas, instruction books. Mail orders. Price list available.)

C. J. BATES AND SONS
Chester, Connecticut 06412

(Color Rak to hold crewel and embroidery yarns, needle threaders, Sure Grip Lip Hoop holds material drumhead tight.)

COATS & CLARK'S CORPORATION
75 Rockefeller Plaza
New York, New York 10019

(Embroidery floss and other yarns.)

THE COUNTING HOUSE
P.O. Box 155
Pawleys Island, South Carolina 29585

(Complete line of cross-stitch supplies; even-weave fabrics, threads. Mail order. Catalog available for 50¢.)

DESIGN A MANIA (Div. of Kleinman Industries)
6909 Eton Ave., Area C
Canoga Park, California 91303

(Counted thread kits.)

ERICA WILSON
717 Madison Avenue
New York, New York

(Needlework supplies, catalog $1.)

KAY & EE CORP. OF AMERICA
200 Fifth Avenue
New York, New York 10010

(Frames, hoops, looms. Price list 25¢.)

NORMARK CORP.
1710 East 78th Street
Minneapolis, Minnesota 55423

(Complete line of scissors.)

SOME PLACE
2990 Adeline Street
Berkeley, California 94703

(An excellent catalog of needlecraft accessories, 25¢.)

STACY FABRICS CORP.
469 Seventh Avenue
New York, New York 10018

(Makers of all-purpose embroidery canvas and multipurpose canvas.)

TAPESTRY
The Galleria
P.O. Box 36161
Houston, Texas 77036
(713) 626-0283

(All types of counted work threads, fabrics. Instruction leaflets and patterns. Write for price list.)

index